SCANDALOUS GRACE

Rediscovering the truth of God's unconditional love, mercy, forgiveness and grace for all people

T. A. Herring

For I am convinced that neither death nor life, neither angels nor demons, neither the present nor the future, nor any powers, neither height nor depth, nor anything else in all creation, will be able to separate us from the love of God that is in Christ Jesus our Lord. (Romans 8:38-39 NIV)

That is why we labor and strive, because we have put our hope in the living God, who is the Savior of all people, and especially of those who believe. (1 Timothy 4:10 NIV)

Dedication

*This book is dedicated to everyone who wonders whether they are worthy of being loved ... or forgiven. To those who despair that their life is unsalvageable from the shipwreck of their mistakes, and who yearn for a life restored to inner peace through love, forgiveness and acceptance by both one's self and, most importantly, by He who has created us all in His own image. It is for those who cling to the last vestiges of hope in an all-encompassing and **Scandalous Grace** that can only come from He who is Love.*

Blessed are the poor in spirit for theirs is the Kingdom of Heaven.

Table of Contents

Why Scandalous Grace?   1

Who Is This Book For and Why Read It?   3

Prologue: The Recent History of Heresies   6

The Intransigence of Tradition   19

How Should We View the Bible?   22

How Do We Know God's Truth?   32

Good News?   40

Are You Saved?   45

The "New" Old Testament   53

Between the Old and New Testaments   69

Hell Facts in the New Testament   71

What Jesus Had to Say About Hell   73

Aion and Aionios in the New Testament   92

Key New Testament Parables   98

Revelation: The Distorted Lens of Biblical Interpretation?   103

Other New Testament Issues   108

A Brief History of the Early Church   113

Universal Reconciliation in the New Testament   129

"Recent" Church History   152

Answering the Arguments Against Universal Reconciliation   159

Conclusion   168

Appendix A Universal Reconciliation Bible Verses   171

Appendix B Early Church Fathers   191

References   199

Acknowledgements   205

SCANDALOUS GRACE

Why Scandalous Grace?

In discussions about God and religion, few things inflame people's passion like the question of what happens after we die. Is there a next life? If so, what is it like? Are there rewards and punishments for what we believed or how we behaved in this life? Does God favor a particular group of people or religion? Most religions have their own unique story and set of beliefs in this regard. Christianity is no different. Sadly, in too many cases, little grace is shown when it comes to God's grace.

History indicates that the notion of *grace* as it relates to man's relationship with God has been around for thousands of years. The scope and inclusiveness of God's grace has been, and is still, at the very core of most religions, and often not in a favorable way. In most cases, God's grace is limited or denied to those who are not like us, or do not believe like we do. However, as history has unfolded and faith traditions have become more enlightened, the moral imperative of accepting, even loving, those who are different from ourselves, even our enemies, has become more and more acknowledged. Most people now embrace the truth of "love the sinner, hate the sin." It is only a short step from this emerging *grace consciousness* in this life to the pregnant, follow-on question of: *What is God's eternal relationship with those who are different from us or do not believe as we do?*

It is my contention that every faith tradition would be well served to reexamine this all-important question that is so central to our relationships in this life and what comes after. When more closely examined, the historical evidence, including the message of Jesus, points to an amazing God of truly *Scandalous Grace*.

Who Is This Book For and Why Read It?

Before answering the above question, let us note that a reference to "the Church" or "Church" within this book refers to the dominant Christian church and its doctrines at the time of the particular subject being discussed.

This book is written primarily for Christians, particularly those Christians who have an earnest desire to better understand how two of the most controversial doctrines of our faith — hell and eternal punishment — relate to Jewish history, the life and teachings of Jesus Christ, the history and evolution of the Christian Church (particularly the first 500-600 years AD), and the Bible. However, it is my sincere desire that anyone searching for truth in these matters, irrespective of their religion, will find this book to be of value in his or her journey.

In many ways this is a book of questions … questions I believe every Christian and seeker of God's truth should ask of themselves, of their beliefs … and of God. It is also a story of history and facts that I believe are unknown, or at least unfamiliar, to many Christians about early Christianity and the Bible. This history and these facts have a direct bearing on current, popular Christian doctrine. It is my conviction that this new information will likely surprise most readers, and is critical to our better understanding of God's essential truth - the truth about His nature, purpose and will.

My goal is to gently encourage all people, and above all Christians, to open their hearts and minds, and undertake their own intellectually honest inquiry of how our beliefs about God have been formed and passed on to us over the millennia.

If you are a traditional Christian, it is my most sincere intention that I not mislead or offend you by this book. I continually pray for guidance that I not be misled in my search for truth, and that I not mislead anyone in his or her quest. My hope and desire is to engage you in a deeper search for truth based upon factual and historical information I suspect may be unknown to you.

Christian doctrine has been dynamic and changing throughout the two millennia since the Church's inception in the first century AD. The Prologue to this book will quickly discuss some significant moral issues on which the Church has only relatively recently reversed itself. All of them have occurred in just the last couple of centuries, and were previously considered grave errors in belief, even heresies, by the Church. Though it may not be every Christian's first thought, these new positions of the Church are a direct reflection of what Christians believe about God's very nature, purpose and will, and what the Church believes the Bible to say.

I realize some Christians may be uncomfortable exploring new or unfamiliar information concerning their beliefs. This is particularly true if our pastors or Christian mentors have not blessed or expressed an opinion on the information first. In considering this book, please keep in mind that our spiritual guides, as earnest and sincere as they may be, may not be fully aware of this information themselves, or have not studied it in depth … or perhaps at all. Many Christian leaders are constrained in their ability to objectively assess or openly embrace the information presented here due to the threat it would impose to their security and status within the institutional church, particularly their very livelihoods.

With this in mind, it is worth contemplating that a mature, informed faith can only be forged in the full awareness of accurate historical facts and Biblical truth. I might humbly suggest that providing your religious counselor(s) a copy of this book would encourage a deeper private spiritual discussion and exchange of ideas that would serve to both refine and fortify your and their faith.

It goes without saying: the conclusions and beliefs you draw from your journey through this book are between you and God. Your spiritual journey, though perhaps facilitated by others, is yours and yours alone. It is my hope this new information will reignite your own spiritual search for and discovery of the truth about God. I will humbly offer my interpretation of various facts and Scripture as appropriate in the context of the topics at hand, but encourage you to conduct your own diligent investigation of all the topics upon which this book touches, and there are many. As to the information, interpretations and conclusions presented in this book, it is my sincerest recommendation that you take what feels right and true, and leave the rest.

Prologue: The Recent History of Heresies

Within the Christian faith, as perhaps other faiths, there is a relatively recent and reoccurring paradox few Christians have likely reflected on for very long, if at all. That paradox is this:

Significant Christian beliefs that were considered dogma for centuries, even millennia, have relatively recently been exposed and discarded as being contrary to the true nature, purpose and will of God. What were long-held orthodox beliefs are now no longer believed, and can only be described as "heresy" according to the "new" orthodox beliefs.

In a nutshell, within the span of the last few centuries, a number of beliefs that were once adamantly condemned as heresy are now considered orthodoxy, and some that were once orthodoxy are now dismissed as heresy.

Have you thought about this relatively recent phenomenon and what it implies? To better understand this enigma of Christian history, let's look at the genesis of the notion of heresy within the Christian faith. We'll also look at a few formerly held beliefs that were long touted as being God-ordained, but today are uniformly viewed as being opposed to the nature, purpose and will of a God who loves all mankind.

The concise definition of "heresy" at the Merriam-Webster Online Dictionary (http://www.merriam-webster.com/dictionary/heresy) is *a belief or opinion that does not agree with the official belief or opinion of a particular religion.*" Many Christians have heard and perhaps used "heresy" to describe beliefs that are at variance with the accepted doctrines of their particular Christian faith. Beginning with the Roman Church in the 5th or 6th century AD, "heresy" and its derivative word "heretic" (one who commits heresy) have been used for over 1500 years to condemn and demonize those who have disagreed with the official doctrines and/or dogma of the Church. By using this most prejudicial of indictments, the "heretical" individual or group is made the object of the strongest possible condemnation and punishment by the Church. Historically, this punishment has ranged from excommunication to death.

According to the Online Etymology Dictionary (http://www.etymonline.com), the origin of the English word "heresy" is from the Latin "hæresis" which in turn was derived from the Greek word "hairesis". According to Thayer and Smith's *The New Testament Greek Lexicon*, the original Greek word *hairesis* meant "a party or sect" in the New Testament. It was used equally to describe the Pharisees, Sadducees and Christians all as "sects" in the Book of Acts. Though these disparate groups clearly embraced differing theological beliefs, *hairesis* itself did not connote harsh condemnation or demonization in its original Biblical context. However, as the word was subsequently translated into the Latin *hairesis*, the Roman Church adapted the word to mean any belief that disagreed with the official dogma of the Roman Church, and any group or person that held such non-conforming beliefs was scathingly declared a "heretic".

From that point forward, the term "heretic" has been used to demonize and ostracize anyone who held or holds a view of God's nature, purpose and will that is at variance with the official position of "the Church" at the time. It is also used to describe any person *believed* to be at variance with the Bible, no matter how sincere or factually correct that person might be. Galileo and his advocacy for Copernican heliocentrism, that the earth was not the center of the universe, is one of the classic examples of the misguided application of the labels "heretic" and "heresy" by the Church to a person and his beliefs that were ultimately determined to be correct, and not in opposition to God or the Bible.

Unfortunately, even today, what is believed to be the "heresy" of "heretics" is often dismissed without even the most cursory examination of the factual, historical or Biblical truthfulness of their claims or arguments. Too frequently a lack of intellectual honesty by the Church's apologists results in a shrill denial of the alleged "heresy" and condemnation of the "heretics" without an objective examination of their assertions, and in many cases ignoring historical facts and/or proper Bible translation and interpretation.

As we will see, various heretics over the centuries have ultimately been determined to be more in tune with God's nature, purpose and will, and the Bible, than the religious establishment of their time. And in many cases their beliefs have eventually become mainstream … i.e. orthodox. What should we make of that?

I am not attempting to dismiss the notion of heresy completely, or to categorically assert that "heretics" are more in tune with God than is the Church. My point is simply this: **The use of the terms "heresy" and "heretic" have too frequently been used by the Church out of a misguided and sometimes disingenuous attempt to shield believers from those beliefs**

perceived as threats to the Church's influence or authority. Instead of an intellectually honest search for truth, dogma and tradition are sometimes reflexively defended without an objective and diligent assessment of the arguments for and against both the traditional Church position and the alternative view.

Let's explore some specific instances of this paradoxical intersection of doctrine and heresy at various points during both Jewish and Christian history.

"Their Hearts Are Far From Me"

> *The Lord says: "These people come near to me with their mouth and honor me with their lips, but their hearts are far from me. Their worship of me is made up only of rules taught by men. (Isaiah 29:13 NIV)*

In the 7th century BC, arguably the greatest of all Old Testament Jewish prophets, Isaiah, was a "lone voice in the wilderness" railing against the sins and unfaithfulness of the Jewish nation. In one of God's most poignant indictments, the Lord tells Isaiah that even though the Jews profess to honor Him, in fact "their hearts are far from me." Instead of honoring and worshipping God by sincerely discerning and following His will and holy commandments in accordance with the Scriptures, the Jews had substituted mere "rules taught by men".

Seven centuries later Jesus refers to this same Scripture when he called the Pharisees and teachers of the law hypocrites.

> *"You hypocrites! Isaiah was right when he prophesied about you: 'These people honor me with their lips, but their hearts are far from me. They worship me in vain; their teachings are but rules taught by men.' "*
> *(Matt 15:7-9, Mark 7:6-7 NIV)*

So what should we draw from these condemnations by Isaiah and Jesus?

One of the clear lessons to be gleaned is that even the supposedly "chosen people" and their religious leaders can misunderstand God for long periods of time, thereby committing real heresy in opposition to His truth, even while thinking themselves righteous and obedient to Him.

"OK, so what relevance," you may be asking, "does this have to today, to me, and to contemporary Christianity?" There is an object lesson all Christians should take to heart from this simple set of Scripture.

Most Christians would assert that Christianity has been the dominant force for good in the world throughout its history, and has been the most prolific and effective agent for spreading peace and goodwill among men. They also would likely attribute this to Christianity's adherence to the Word of God, i.e. the Bible. While this is certainly true in part, and particularly if one only looks at the Christian position on certain key moral issues *a posteriori* (after the fact), the historical Christian record *a priori* (before the fact) is a somewhat different story.

Sadly and throughout far too much of the Christian era, the Bible, represented as "God's Word", has too often been invoked to rationalize and perpetuate shameful iniquity and cruelty in conjunction with maintaining the status quo … the exact antithesis for which Jesus gave his life. This abuse and misuse of the Bible in the name of "Christian doctrine" first began in the 5th century when the Western Church became an instrument of the Roman Empire. Consider the following.

Christian Persecution of Heretics

Beginning in the 5th century AD (shortly after the Roman Empire became the Western Church), people deemed as "heretics" by the Church began to be persecuted, tortured and even murdered. This practice accelerated in the 6th century AD under Roman Emperor Justinian, the political and de facto clerical head of the Church at that time, and continued for more than 1000 years (known as the "Dark Ages"), becoming particularly insidious during the various Inquisitions of the late Middle Ages. However, the aggressive physical punishment and psychological castigation of "heretics" continued even into the modern era in what became the Protestant branch of Christianity, only beginning to wane as recently as the 18th century AD. The institutional punishment of perceived heresies via condemnation and excommunication continues today in some segments of Christendom.

Christian Persecution of Jews

Throughout much or most of the 2000-year Christian era, Jews were regarded as heretical "Christ killers", and were persecuted and even killed in the name of both God and Jesus, with the implicit or explicit sanctioning of the Church. In spite of the teachings of the Apostle Paul, the acceptance of Jews (or at least a remnant of 144,000 as prophesied in the book of Revelation) as co-heirs in the kingdom of God (see Rom 11:25-32) is a relatively recent, 20th century Christian phenomenon. In fact, it is possible that had it not been for the Holocaust, Christians today might still be discriminating against or persecuting Jews in a most un-Christ-like fashion.

Christian Enslavement of Non-Christians

Only within the last 300 years have many Christian nations and the Church as a whole come to understand that God does not sanction humans owning or controlling other humans as slaves, chattel or otherwise. Sadly, the view that non-Christians are equally beloved children of God was declared to be heresy by the Church for many centuries, and a small minority of Christians still clings to this position today.

Until the mid-18th century AD, many Christians accepted slavery, particularly the enslavement of non-Christians. In fact, the spreading of the Christian Gospel (i.e. the Great Commission) played a key and tragic role in the colonization of entire countries and continents around the globe, and the subjugation and enslavement of the indigent peoples. This episode in Western Christian history is one of the saddest and darkest episodes in the less than perfect history of our faith.

Today, virtually all Christians are solidly united in the condemnation of slavery as immoral and in clear opposition to God's will, even though sadly some Christians would still deny the equal love for all in the eyes of God. As a somewhat ironic aside, the United States, arguably the most Christian of present-day nations, was one of the later Christian societies to outlaw slavery and officially condemn it.

Christian Oppression of People of Color, Women and Other Religions

Within many "Christian nations" (or formerly Christian nations), only during the last century have people of color, women and other non-Christian religious groups (e.g. Jews, Muslims, Hindus, Buddhists, etc.) begun to receive the same rights and opportunities that have historically been provided only to white and/or male Christians. This historical oppression, discrimination and segregation was perpetrated with the tacit sanction of the institutional Christian Church … until it finally became clear that the vast majority of earlier Christians and the Church had misunderstood Jesus' teachings and the Bible … and that these injustices were clearly not what God intended.

With regard to each of the above moral disgraces, history clearly records it was from within the Bible (principally, but not exclusively, in the Old Testament) that the Church and most Christians, at least initially, found the rationale and doctrine for the then-existing immoral and unjust social order and human rights abuses. It was the moral conscience and reason of a minority of enlightened men and women, among them Christians, who found themselves at odds with official Church doctrine, which served as the catalyst for re-examining and ultimately overturning the then traditional Biblical understanding.

One might wonder from where, in the face of staunch Church resistance, did this enlightenment come? Though one might speculate numerous explanations and sources, in the end it would seem the only plausible explanation is that *God Himself must have inspired it.*

After almost two thousand years of misunderstanding God on these key issues, and finding support for that error in His Word, God's will concerning the universal dignity and rights of all people finally overcame the darkness that had concealed the light of His truth. After the fact, most Christians have come to see the Biblical source for God's belatedly revealed love for all people, and righteous anger at man's immoral acts and injustices perpetrated in His name. Given this, it is VERY important to note: **God did not change … only man's understanding of Him.**

In light of the Church's and most Christians' failure to glean from the Bible what later became clear and accepted truths regarding God's will on some of history's most significant human rights issues, there are several questions one might ask:

- What caused the Christian Church to be on the wrong side of history on these critical moral issues in the first place?

- Having only reversed its doctrinal positions on these important human rights issues within the past few centuries, how certain should we NOW be that current Church doctrine is absolutely correct on other issues regarding God's nature, purpose and will?

- What do the Church's new doctrinal positions on these key moral issues say about God? Do they portray a more or less gracious image of our Heavenly Father?

- How should we weigh current Christian doctrine against our own conscience as it relates to what we believe about God's nature, purpose and will?

- If a doctrine or teaching of the Church "doesn't feel right", or is at odds with our conscience or reason, what should we do?

I strongly believe each person should reflect on these questions and what they might say about "orthodox Christian doctrine" and "truth" as declared by the institutional Church, our particular Christian denomination, and even our pastor.

Slavery – A Critical Biblical Conundrum

In order to weigh the above questions and ultimately arrive at a comfortable moral resting spot, I believe it is helpful to consider why the Church and most Christians were wrong for most of the Christian era with regard to the particular issue of slavery. Based upon an objective reading of the Bible, the reason would appear to be rather straightforward: **The Bible does not condemn slavery, but explicitly accepts it as part of the normal social order.**

Though some Christians might disagree, the relevant Scriptures seem fairly clear. Here are a few, most from the New Testament.

> *Your male and female slaves are to come from the nations around you; from them you may buy slaves. (Lev 25:44 NIV)*
>
> *If a man sells his daughter as a female slave, she is not to go free as the male slaves do. (Exodus 21:7 NASB)*
>
> *Slaves, obey your earthly masters with respect and fear, and with sincerity of heart, just as you would obey Christ. (Eph 6:5 NIV)*
>
> *And masters, treat your slaves in the same way. Do not threaten them, since you know that he who is both their Master and yours is in heaven, and there is no favoritism with him. (Eph 6:9 NIV)*
>
> *Slaves, obey your earthly masters in everything; and do it, not only when their eye is on you and to win their favor, but with sincerity of heart and reverence for the Lord. (Col 3:22 NIV)*
>
> *Masters, provide your slaves with what is right and fair, because you know that you also have a Master in heaven. (Col 4:1 NIV)*
>
> *All who are under the yoke of slavery should consider their masters worthy of full respect, so that God's name and our teaching may not be slandered. (1 Tim 6:1 NIV)*
>
> *Teach slaves to be subject to their masters in everything, to try to please them, not to talk back to them, (Tit 2:9 NIV)*

> *Slaves, submit yourselves to your masters with all re-*
> *spect, not only to those who are good and considerate,*
> *but also to those who are harsh. (1 Pet 2:18 NIV)*

Though the above verses encourage masters to provide their slaves "with what is right and fair" and "do not threaten them", they clearly do not speak against the practice of slavery in any manner whatsoever. To the contrary, they accept it as part of the normal social order. [One should ponder how this fact is reconciled with the concepts of God's immutability and the Bible's presumed infallibility by many Christians.] It is for this reason, among others, that Christians and the Church found Biblical justification for slavery for the better part of two thousand years after Christ, and his apostles, repeatedly commanded us to *"Love your neighbor as yourself." (Matt 19:19, 22:39; Mark 12:31, 12:33; Luke 10:27; Rom 13:9; Gal 5:14; James 2:8 NIV)*. Apart from the commandment to love God with all our heart, soul and strength, this is arguably the most prolific commandment in the entire Bible.

In answer to the question "Who is my neighbor?" Christ responded with the parable of the Good Samaritan (Luke 10:29-37) that tells us all people, even our supposed enemies (as the Samaritans were to the faithful Jews of the time), are our neighbors. This seeming contradiction of loving "your neighbor" (i.e. all people) with the slave verses quoted above is admittedly confusing unless one contends Jesus did not mean a slave was to be considered "our neighbor". If we are to love our neighbors as ourself and to *"Do to others as you would have them do to you." (Luke 6:31 NIV)*, as Christ commanded, which of us would want to be enslaved by our neighbor? As heinous as all of this now sounds to our enlightened mind, the Church and most Christians concluded that slaves were not their "neighbors" for most of the Christian era. And in spite of Paul's proclamation regarding slaves and their masters in Eph

6:9 ("there is no favoritism with him [God]"), they were not viewed as having equal standing in the eyes of men or God. They were viewed as subhuman ... worthy only of enslavement ... and certainly not equal children of God.

Implications for Today

In light of the Church's past errors in misunderstanding God's nature, purpose and will, and its relatively recent reversals on long-held orthodox beliefs now deemed unworthy of God, many people might wonder if current Church doctrine may still reflect similar misunderstandings. If that could conceivably be true, is it not incumbent upon every Christian to engage in an intellectually honest examination of key Christian doctrines that may be at variance with our God-given conscience to see if they are decisively supported by Biblical and historical facts and reason?

Every person must come to their own answers on these important matters of faith. However, it may be helpful to consider that the Prophets, Jesus, the Apostles and Disciples, and the fathers of the Reformation, all came down on the side of following the small, inner voice of God in searching for His truth. All of them were "heretics" in their time. Contrary to the accusations of their enemies, they didn't disregard Scripture ... they found new meaning and truth within it ... and always a more gracious and loving God, even if not yet then the full, unconditional embodiment of "God is love" as expressed by John the Apostle.

Hell – The Final Orthodox Heresy?

With this more gracious and loving God in mind, many sincere Christians are reexamining the doctrines of hell and eternal punishment in the light of Church history, more accurate Biblical translation and interpretation, and our God-given conscience and reason. It is my contention that in the not-too-distant future this Dark Age dogma will be exposed as a misguided slur against the love of God for all His children, and a tragic libel against Him. I submit that Christians everywhere will one day be uniformly appalled that such an abhorrent belief about our unconditionally loving and merciful Father could have infiltrated our faith and been ascribed as having been taught by Jesus Christ himself. The previous claims of our well-intended Christian ancestors who unwittingly promulgated this pagan notion of God will be exposed, like previous abandoned doctrine, as having been based on flawed scriptural interpretations of God's nature, purpose and will.

The remainder of this book is dedicated to the search for the truth about the limits, if any, on God's love, mercy, forgiveness and grace. A search for truth that too many professing Christians may automatically condemn as *scandalous* before our investigation even begins. Echoing the rigidity and narrow-mindedness of the Church of the Middle Ages, some might even label this search as heresy or blasphemy. I can only wonder if God really objects to our desire to better understand His heart.

The Intransigence of Tradition

Most people would agree that personal habits developed over many years can be very hard to break. For many people, some physical habits are clearly harmful – smoking, eating unhealthy foods, a sedentary lifestyle, ancsthctizing our mind and bodies with alcohol and drugs, etc. – yet they continue to do them anyway. Of course, there are mental habits that can be equally destructive – lack of self confidence, low self esteem, negative thinking patterns, narcissism, infidelity, kleptomania, gambling addiction, etc. Usually it is only with great effort, and often outside help, that most people are able to overcome long-held personal habits that are detrimental to their physical or mental health, or relationships. As you might imagine, undesirable habits that are not as clearly detrimental to our physical or mental health or relationships can be even harder to break because the incentive to do so is often unclear.

Like people, organizations and institutions also have "habits", both good and bad, usually referred to as "traditions". In the case of the Christian Church, traditions are rooted in apostolic or Church history, or in Biblical scripture itself. Like personal habits, some Church traditions are more meaningful and worthwhile than others. Many are benign and simply embody cherished rituals. Others involve specific beliefs, usually referred to as doctrine or, depending upon their verifiability and rigidity, dogma.

One of the unusual aspects of some Church traditions and doctrines is that over the span of centuries and millennia their foundations have been obscured by their origins in antiquity and the fog of history. As a result, the modern basis for them becomes something closely akin to dogma. That is, the particular belief is asserted to be true with less than clear, objective proof or supporting rationale. In short, it is accepted solely on faith, often dismissing critical questioning or examination.

After centuries of advocacy and enforcement by the Church, a doctrine or tradition can become deeply entrenched and highly intransigent, resisting reform efforts for decades and centuries. Just the act of factually and rationally questioning it can be discouraged as heresy. As has been discussed elsewhere, for much of the Christian era that was the case with issues like slavery, segregation, and both racial and women's rights and equality, among others. That was the way things had always been and faithful Christians were told by the clergy for more than 1000 years that was what the Bible said, so it was not necessary, or permitted, to question those issues. After all, God had revealed Himself long ago on these topics ... hadn't He?

So what should we do when Church traditions are challenged or brought into question?

Based upon history, there clearly are times when the Church should step back and reexamine certain long-held traditions and beliefs in the face of new evidence that perhaps the nature, purpose and will of God has been misinterpreted or misunderstood. Neither the Church nor we should get defensive or hostile when these situations occur. After all, in many cases it is not God who is being challenged, but man's flawed understanding of God and the Bible that are being called into question.

As discussed in the Prologue, this was the case with the Church's almost 2000-year persecution of heretics and Jews, slavery, and the denial of rights and discrimination against other religions, races and women. It is our strong belief the modern-day Christian doctrines of hell and eternal punishment fall into this same category of man's misunderstanding God over a long period of time. And like a long-held bad habit, many Christians do not want to hear about it, acknowledge it, or reexamine it from an objective and intellectually honest standpoint. However, as Jesus said,

> "If you hold to my teaching, you are really my disciples. Then you will know the truth, and the truth will set you free." (John 8:31-32 NIV)

With this in mind, it is our belief that all people, and in particular all Christians, should strive with all their might to truly understand and hold to Jesus' teachings so we will know the truth and be set free. **And could there be any more pressing matter of truth than for us to come to our most sincere and certain faith concerning the love our Heavenly Father has for all mankind ... and His eternal plan for us all?**

How Should We View the Bible?

At some point, most people have heard one or more of the following claims made regarding the Bible.

> *"The Holy Bible is the inspired, inerrant and infallible Word of God."*
>
> *"The Bible contains all truth."*
>
> *"If any of it is not true, then none of it is true."*

There is no question the Bible, and what it is believed to say, has been the lynchpin of the Christian faith since the inception of the Bible canon in the late 4th century AD. But, as we have already discussed, both the Church and most Christians have at times demonstrably misunderstood the Bible with respect to certain key moral issues. In spite of this, the above statements, and others like them, reflect the revered and exalted status of the Bible within Christendom, particularly the more conservative segments of Christianity.

There is an interesting dynamic around the Bible that is worth briefly discussing. The vast majority of Christians only begin to read and study the Bible AFTER they have adopted a particular set of theological and doctrinal beliefs, generally those of their church, pastor, parents, friends, or favorite Christian writers. They have already been exposed to certain passages of Scripture and the particular interpretation of those passages based upon the influence of their Christian mentors and colleagues. The consequence of this is that when they do begin their investigation into the Bible they have in many cases been conditioned to read it in a manner that simply validates what they already believe. In addition, if they use Bible study guides, they tend to only use those that are consistent with the set of doctrinal beliefs they already hold. In a very real sense, they are afraid that deviating from this theological path is dangerous, even heresy. The net result is that many Christians never undertake their own search for the underlying meaning of various portions of the Bible, or the overarching message of the Bible as a whole. They compliantly accept the interpretation that has been passed on to them, in many cases even in light of reservations they might have about what they perceive to be inconsistencies between various portions of Scripture or in the very image of God they hold.

In light of the central role the Bible plays in many people's fear of stepping outside the theological and doctrinal boundaries by which they often feel constrained, it is worth briefly reflecting on the Bible's factual history to remove some of its mystique; to better understand how it was created and has evolved; and what other leading Christian figures thought about it. With this in mind, the following are some pertinent facts about the Bible to keep in mind.

- The Bible was written over approximately 1500-2000 years (no one knows for sure; this is just an educated guess) by more than 40 (again not precisely known) human authors, many or most of whom are not definitively known other than through Jewish and/or Christian tradition.

- The "Jewish Bible" (or Tanakh) that comprises the various books of the Old Testament was originally written in Hebrew.

- The books of the New Testament were originally written in Koine Greek, the *lingua franca* of the eastern Mediterranean world from the time of its conquest by Alexander the Great (356-323 BC). Greek was the universal written language of the New Testament authors during the first century AD, as well as for the literate early Christians who read these writings during the first several centuries before Christianity became the official religion of the Roman Empire in the 4th century AD.

- *There are no surviving original manuscripts of any of the books of the Old or New Testaments.* All we have are copies, the earliest of which were made hundreds of years following the original writings. The oldest surviving manuscripts date to the 3rd and 4th centuries AD.

- The first translation of the Hebrew Bible was into Greek following Alexander's conquest of that part of the world in the 4th century BC. The name given to this translation is the Septuagint. It is often simply referred to by the Roman numeral LXX by Bible scholars. Tradition has it that 70 expert scholars (or 72 depending on which story you accept) knowledgeable in both Hebrew and Greek each made independent translations of the Hebrew Scriptures to ensure the best possible translation to the Greek language. According to this tradition all of the copies were identical and the translation was done sometime during the period 275-100 BC.

- Over the centuries there have been and still are some differences of opinion as to which specific books should comprise the Old Testament. This dispute revolves around the status of a number of Old Testament books called the Apocrypha (from the Greek word meaning "those having been hidden away"). These books have been both included and excluded from the "official" Old Testament canon at different points in time. Up until the end of the 19th century, all or most Protestant Bibles included them, but now exclude them. This will likely surprise most Christians.

- There is no single copy of the New Testament that is deemed to be the authoritative Greek source from which all subsequent translations of the Bible are derived or have been made. In fact, today there are approximately 5,700 different ancient Greek copies or fragments of various portions of the New Testament. This number continues to increase as new archeological discoveries are made. As recently as the early 18th century, there were approximately only 80 ancient Greek copies or fragments of the New Testament that were generally known at that time. An Oxford scholar named John Mill (circa 1707) spent 30 years analyzing this group of ancient New Testament copies/fragments. He identified and catalogued more than 30,000 variations or discrepancies in the text across these different sources, some of them significant with respect to how the Bible had been historically understood up to that time.

- The official Bible canon (i.e. the specific books that came to comprise the Bible) was not established until the late 4th and early 5th centuries after Rome adopted Christianity as its official religion. The official canon was defined at various ecumenical councils of church leaders held over the course of approximately 40 years beginning around 367 AD. Though a number of different Gospels had been circulating among early Christians during the first several centuries, there had developed a general consensus that the four primary Gospels–Matthew, Mark, Luke and John–represented the authentic Christian tradition. However, there were differences of opinion among church leaders with respect to some of the other epistles or books of the New Testament, but ultimately an official canon was established by majority vote that included the Apocrypha as part of the Old Testament. Nevertheless, some books were more controversial than others. For example, the Book of Revelation was included in the canon by a contentious and relatively close vote.

- Historical evidence suggests that approximately 60% of early Church fathers viewed Revelation as authentic and authoritative while the other 40% did not. However, even among those Church elders who accepted it, there were significant differences as to its meaning, with most appearing to favor a symbolic versus literal interpretation.

- Upon general agreement of the Bible canon by the Roman Church, authorities then set out to create the first comprehensive Latin translation of what subsequently became the Bible. However, as a result of the numerous Roman persecutions of both

Christians and Jews, and the associated destruction of their writings, up until the early 4th century AD, it is virtually certain that no original Hebrew or Greek manuscripts existed by that time, only copies of their sacred writings. Consequently, this early Latin Bible translation was based upon copies, not originals. The translation work was both directed by and significantly performed by one man, St. Jerome. It was completed at various stages over roughly the same period of time as the finalization of the Bible canon. The result of this early translation effort was called the Latin Vulgate Bible and became the official Bible of the Roman Church over the next several centuries, enduring even to the present as the official Latin Bible of the Catholic Church. As we will discuss later, evidence suggests some key translation issues and/or errors crept into Scripture when the Greek copies of the New Testament books were translated into Latin.

- For approximately the next 1000 years, the Latin Vulgate Bible was the only Bible available in the Roman Church, and for most of this period only members of the clergy were allowed to possess or read it ... under the possible penalty of death! Since most people couldn't read anyway, this may or may not have been a significant issue. However, it did reflect the attitude that the Church officially positioned itself between God and man as God's divinely appointed interpreter, mediator and earthly representative. By the 6th century, the Roman emperor and later the pope assumed the role as God's surrogate on earth.

- In the late 15th century, the first copies of Greek New Testament manuscripts began to find their way into Western Europe around the same time as dissatisfaction with the corrupt teachings and practices of the Roman Catholic Church began to surface. When Thomas Linacre, an Oxford Greek scholar, began to compare these Greek manuscript copies with the Latin Bible he declared, "Either this [the original Greek] is not the Gospel... or we are not Christians," highlighting both the discrepancies between the Latin Bible and the Greek manuscripts and the deviation of the Roman Church from Biblical principles.

- As the Reformation movement and rising literacy in the middle class began to gather steam in the 15th and 16th centuries, public sentiment began to build to have the Latin Bible translated into other languages. The Roman Catholic Church strictly forbade this, again under penalty of death. In spite of this, English (or more accurately Olde English), German and other translations began to be made by hand. This translation effort gained significant momentum with the invention of Johannes Gutenberg's movable type printing press in the mid-15th century. Several Bibles were translated from the Latin Vulgate, but with the growing availability of Hebrew and Greek copies of the Scriptures, Protestant Bibles began to be increasingly based on these other sources that were deemed to be more "authentic". Unfortunately, these "native" language sources were only several centuries old themselves, and more than a thousand years later than the actual Bible authors' original writings.

- There were a number of Bible translations created during the 15th, 16th and 17th centuries – the Tynedale Bible, the Coverdale Bible, the Mathews

Bible, the Geneva Bible, the Bishop's Bible, and the Douay-Rheims Catholic English Bible (after much gnashing of teeth by the Roman Church) to name a few. However, in 1611 the King James Bible was first published after having been commissioned by King James I of England to be "the translation to end all translations". The King James Bible was strongly based upon the Latin Vulgate Bible and a small number of available Greek texts called the Textus Receptus, which were only a few centuries old themselves. King James instructed the KJV translators to create a translation that did not contradict the then accepted orthodox Biblical interpretation, particularly as it pertained to the divine right of kings that was being questioned with ever-greater frequency. Over the course of the next several decades, the King James Bible became the official English Protestant Bible and held this position for over 400 years and well into the twentieth century.

- Such imminent Christian authorities and fathers of the Reformation as Martin Luther and John Calvin questioned the official Bible canon as recently as the 16th century. Luther, along with some Catholic theologians, attempted to have the books of Hebrews, James, Jude and Revelation removed from the New Testament canon. He also excised the deutero-canonical books from the Catholic Old Testament, calling them "Apocrypha … books which are not considered equal to the Holy Scriptures, but are useful and good to read". In addition, he unsuccessfully tried to have the Old Testament book of Esther classified as Apocrypha since it never mentions God.

- John Calvin also had issues with the "authority" of several New Testament books, among them Hebrews and James. In addition, though It appears he may have believed Revelation to be canonical, it is one of only three New Testament books, including 2nd and 3rd John, on which he did not write a commentary. However, historical evidence indicates that Luther, Calvin and most of the reformers of their time held a distinctly different understanding of Revelation (as did many/most early Church fathers, e.g. Augustine, etc.) than the more conservative, Bible-centric segment of Christianity today. It is generally agreed the Protestant reformers of Luther and Calvin's era held what is now called a *historical amillenial* view of Revelation, not the *dispensational premillenial* view held by more conservative Christians today. This will be discussed further later, though essentially this is an argument as to whether the 1000 year earthly reign of Christ allegedly prophesied in the Bible was a symbolic reference and is synonymous with the current church age or whether it will be an actual 1000 year reign by Christ himself on earth beginning at some future time.

• Beginning in the late 19th century, a number of modern Bible translations began to be created, many or most of which were based upon more recently discovered and older copies of Old and New Testament Hebrew and Greek manuscripts that were deemed to be more representative of what the original Scripture authors actually wrote (though no original copies actually exist). This set of reference manuscripts is commonly referred to as the *Majority Text*. A few of the more common of these modern translations, and some to which we will subsequently refer in this book, are:

- English Revised Version (1885)
- Young's Literal Translation (1898)
- American Standard Version (1901)
- Revised Standard Version (1952, 1971)
- New International Version (1973, 1978, 1984, 2011)
- New King James (1982)
- New American Standard Bible (1995)
- Today's New International Version (2001, 2005)
- As a result of the older and different source documents from which these translations were derived, there are differences in what various Bibles "say" with respect to several key issues.

We have now laid down a somewhat streamlined and factual history of the origins and transmission of the Bible over the millennia, and some of the different translations used by various factions within Christendom. With this understanding, we might ask the following questions:

- If the Bible is the "inspired, inerrant and infallible Word of God", what are we to make of leading Christian figures throughout history questioning the authority of at least some portions of Scripture?
- How have certain segments of the Church come to view the Bible as the sole source of God's truth?
- And perhaps most importantly, if there have been different interpretations of Scripture throughout the history of the Church, how can we now be confident that we absolutely know God's truth once and for all?

How Do We Know God's Truth?

What we believe, or don't, about God is perhaps the most vital of all human understandings. It is at the very heart of what is good and gracious about the human race, as well as much of the evil that has been perpetrated by man in the name of God. In the eloquent words of Dr. Loyal Hurley,

> *"The most important thinking in the world is the thinking men do about God. True ideas of God lead to nobility of life; false ideas of God lead to the opposite."*

The atrocities committed by men of the Church in the name of God and rationalized using the Bible over the two millennia since the life and death of Jesus are testimony to what happens when men harbor false ideas about God. Given the historical difficulty even the Church has experienced in knowing the truth about God's nature, purpose and will, I believe we should all ponder the following question: **What do we really know about God's truth and how do we come to know it?**

Sola Scriptura

For many Christians, the answer to the preceding question is immediate and obvious … *all* knowledge of God's nature, purpose and will is derived *solely* from the Bible. In this view, the Bible **IS** the inerrant, inspired and infallible Word of God revealed to and written by man. This absolute primacy of Scripture was called "sola scriptura" (Latin for "by Scripture alone") by the reformers who spawned the Protestant Reformation. Under this view and at a personal level, God's will is revealed through study of Biblical Scripture and prayer, both occurring in consultation with the Holy Spirit. In this view, the Holy Spirit may "speak" to us by whatever means, but it is only deemed to be genuinely "from God" if it conforms to orthodox Biblical doctrine. Any contradictory guidance must be from Satan.

In theory, this primacy of the Bible excludes all other avenues of revelation about the nature, purpose and will of God. In practice, Bible studies, books and narratives that enlighten Scripture *and are consistent with accepted doctrine* are viewed as speaking truth and perhaps as inspired, though certainly not on the same level as the Bible.

In this view it is obviously paramount that one be absolutely certain he or she accurately understands what the *original* Bible Scriptures say, both in isolation and in context. Given that, one might infer that all Scripture must harmonize to present a coherent and consistent image of God's nature, purpose and will. Somewhat ironically, though some Christians would disagree, the relatively recent development of *dispensational theology* over the past 200+ years (as a response to claims of inconsistency within the Bible) has rationalized away the need for consistency within Scripture to a significant degree.

Irrespective of contemporary Christianity's view of Scripture, the abundant evidence of the past doctrinal errors and injustices, committed both by the Church as a whole and Christians individually, demonstrate the great difficulty man has in understanding and living in accordance with the truth of God's nature, purpose and will as revealed within the Bible.

Extra-Biblical Inspiration

For other equally sincere Christians, the answer to the question of how we come to know God's truth is not as clear-cut. Though they believe the Bible CONTAINS (as opposed to IS) the inspired word of God and is the original and primary source of knowledge about God's nature, purpose and will, these more freethinking Christians do not believe the Bible is the only means by which we may come to know His truth. This perspective holds that God continues to reveal Himself to man through various means including:

- personal experiences or encounters with God, presumably via the Holy Spirit; and
- inspired insights derived from nature, literature, art, or other spiritually discerning persons, all arguably inspired by the Holy Spirit.

Under this view, these supplementary avenues of inspiration can cast new light on Scripture or clarify truth about God that has previously been unrecognized, or unacknowledged, by some portions of the Church and perhaps many Christians.

A modern-day example of this extra-Biblical inspiration is our recent "enlightenment" regarding the civil rights of persons of color. Given his significant role in this relatively recent illumination within our society, who would seriously argue that Dr. Martin Luther King's belief in peaceful resistance (per Christ's example) and his 1963 *"I Have A Dream"* speech were not divinely inspired in some form or fashion? Ironically,

Dr. King's inspiration came from the same Bible much of the Church at the time believed endorsed the inequality of and denial of equal rights to people of color, particularly non-Christians. Unfortunately, many if not most white Christians could not see God's truth of the equality of all people until Dr. King poignantly expressed the love and grace our Father has for all of His children, and gently reminded us we are commanded by Jesus to love our neighbors regardless of race, creed, color … or religion.

It is worth noting that since the beginning of the Protestant Reformation in the 16th century, alternative images of God that later became accepted doctrine have invariably described a more merciful, inclusive and loving Father than the prevailing doctrine of the time.

This observation might make one wonder if the Reformation is not still an ongoing process, as opposed to a relatively recent historical event.

Though there are undoubtedly numerous variants of the above two perspectives of how we arrive at our beliefs about God and His essential truth, these two positions generally capture the most essential differences in competing contemporary Christian worldviews.

The Mind of God

In addition to the inherent difficulty of understanding the truth about God, there is another question we must consider: **Is it an oxymoron to claim to know, as most religions do, the mind and truth of an infinite God?**

Even if one accepts the Bible as the inspired Word of God, the fact remains it is undeniably finite. It contains a fixed set of Scripture. Though this Scripture can, as we have seen, be interpreted to contain different understandings of God's nature, purpose and will, the end result is these interpretations are still finite in content and number. Given this, consider this simple question: **Can a finite Bible, even though inspired, fully encompass the mind of an infinite God?**

I believe a rational person must seriously consider this apparent paradox, particularly taking into account the historical evidence as to how specific erroneous beliefs have influenced Christian doctrine. This history and the associated facts surrounding early Christianity and the Bible are the subject of the remainder of this book.

Knowing the Bible and God

At this point, I would respectfully and humbly like to make the following assertion.

Rational inquiry and reasoning applied to Biblical scripture are NOT inconsistent with Christian faith. Indeed, it is the obligation of every sincere Christian to engage in an intellectually honest search for truth about God's nature, purpose and will. It is only by earnestly undertaking this quest that we will truly bring glory to God.

As God himself is perfect and immutable, then He must be perfectly rational and perfectly reliable, among His many other perfect attributes. Can anyone imagine worshipping a capricious god who acts indiscriminately under identical moral circumstances? *This world and our faith would be utterly incomprehensible and disheartening if a god that is anything other than perfectly rational and reliable rules the universe.*

In considering the question of how we come to our beliefs concerning the nature, purpose and will of our infinite Father, there are two additional questions every Christian should ponder:

1. How thorough is our personal Biblical knowledge upon which we base our beliefs about God?

2. In light of Biblically rationalized injustices throughout history, including the modern era, how certain should we NOW be that we fully understand what the Bible says about God?

Since the beginning of the Christian era and particularly since the Reformation, there have been countless disagreements by sincere Christians as to precisely what the *original* Scriptures say. The incontrovertible evidence of this phenomenon is the more than 38,000 Christian denominations and hundreds of Bible translations that exist today. These denominations are principally differentiated by how they interpret the Bible as to what it says about God's nature, purpose and will.

How Certain Should We Be?

Given the inherently finite nature of Scripture and the widely disparate views over what it says that have existed since the time of the apostles, it would seem prudent for all Christians to humbly continue reminding themselves of Jesus' words when he was chastising the self-righteous religious leaders in Jerusalem.

> *Thus you nullify the word of God for the sake of your tradition. You hypocrites! Isaiah was right when he prophesied about you: 'These people honor me with their lips, but their hearts are far from me. They worship me in vain; their teachings are but rules taught by men.' (Matt 15:7-9)*

According to Jesus, we can "***nullify the word of God***" by putting tradition (i.e. man-made rules) before truth. Adopting a position of absolute certitude as to the nature, purpose and will of an infinite God may find us guilty of the same self-righteousness and misguided legalism Jesus condemned in the religious establishment of his time. Though we should strive for a strong faith in the nature and purpose of God, our faith must walk a fine line between overly confident self-assurance on the one hand, and being a sincere and gracious seeker of truth on the other.

According to Jesus, our faith must not devolve into limiting God to man-made rules, or a book, that can mirror the human imperfections of those who created, compiled, translated and interpreted it, and then insist "true believers" must adhere to the resulting dogma or doctrine created by imperfect and fallible men. This was precisely the error the Jewish religious establishment made in Isaiah's and Jesus' times, and for which both so vehemently condemned them.

This was also the same indictment made by Martin Luther, John Calvin and the other fathers of the Reformation against the Roman Catholic Church in medieval times. The Catholic Church had fallen into both theological error and corruption. It had strayed far from the Bible. Human imperfections in the character and integrity of the Catholic power structure in the Middle Ages led to significant distortions and misrepresentations of God's nature, purpose and will, resulting in such unconscionable practices as the selling of indulgences by priests.

God's truth, as we have seen, has been misunderstood and abused multiple times by those claiming exclusivity in knowing Him. Given this recurring historical pattern which has occurred even within recent decades, is it so hard to conceive that contemporary Christianity could make similar misjudgments in its understanding of God today? History and experience attest that this is at least a possibility.

Where men are involved, it should not automatically be considered an offense to Christian faith to say it may happen again ... or may be happening today. Consequently, we are called to be ever vigilant not to be inadvertent participants in theological miscalculation like our Christian predecessors. The search for God's truth requires us to question and verify all that might seemingly conflict with our most noble ideas of God or His image within us. We must not simply accept difficult to reconcile or illogical doctrine because it has been passed down as part of the tradition of our particular denomination.

Lest anyone take offense to the preceding assertions, I urge you to keep in mind the rich tradition begun by the Old Testament prophets, Jesus and his disciples–and followed by the apostles, the early church fathers, and the initiators of the Protestant Reformation–in questioning whether the institutionally mandated understanding of God's nature, purpose and will of their time was in fact the ultimate truth about God.

Good News?

You may be wondering why I'm so concerned that Christians today critically assess the traditional orthodox Christian doctrine of hell and eternal punishment prior to simply accepting it as the final word on God's truth. Apart from my strong conviction that our spiritual journey and relationship with God are richly enhanced by a sincere quest for truth, there's another reason.

I believe it can be compellingly demonstrated that our Heavenly Father's love and grace for all mankind are more merciful and noble than Christianity has traditionally depicted.

This claim is based upon factual and generally unfamiliar early Christian church history, the Bible, and what many Hebrew and Greek scholars contend are critical mistranslations of a few key words in the original Old and New Testament Scriptures.

One might intuitively think this is good news (no pun intended) ... a Heavenly Father whose love for all of His children is even more magnificent than we previously thought! Wouldn't that be GREAT news? Is God not wonderful!

Well … sadly … and somewhat surprisingly … I've discovered this isn't such good news to some Christians. You might be asking yourself, like I did, "Why would not all Christians be open to and joyous about an even more loving, gracious God?" Many people find this confusing, and seemingly contradictory with the uniquely Christian notion of "God is love." (1 John 4:8, 16)

After much inquiry and soul searching, I humbly believe I have come to an explanation why many sincere Christians might feel this way today. To put it as respectfully and delicately as possible, *I think it is the unintentional product of:*

1. a confusing Church tradition [based on what will be shown to be a faulty interpretation of Scripture] of "conditional" grace, but usually asserted to be "unconditional";
2. the institutional investment in centuries of tradition and doctrine making any shift or change a monumental undertaking;
3. man's innate propensity toward false pride which disposes us to unconsciously and incongruously believe we are deserving of God's unconditional grace; and
4. a distorted view and prioritization of God's "justice" over His unconditional love.

This unwholesome combination has resulted in a propensity toward rigid Church dogma that has stifled a thorough and intellectually honest search for truth in the full light of facts, history, informed Biblical translation and interpretation, and God's continuing divine inspiration via the Holy Spirit.

Christianity's less than totally gracious view of God's nature, purpose and will as it pertains to the ultimate destiny of mankind has its institutional roots in both Judaism immediately prior to and concurrent with Jesus ministry, and Roman Emperor Constantine's 4th century AD usurpation of Christianity by the previously pagan Roman Empire. Try to imagine literally millions of pagan Roman citizens (and priests?) who had previously worshiped a pantheon of capricious and angry gods becoming "Christians" essentially by imperial edict as opposed to authentic spiritual conversion. An interesting and somewhat parallel illustration of this phenomenon is Augustine himself, one of the most revered early Roman Church theologians, who had been a Manichean prior to his conversion to Christianity. Manicheans believed in a perpetual dualistic battle between good and evil at work within the world and men, and denied the existence of an omnipotent god able to defeat evil. This Manichean theology of a less-than-omnipotent god eliminated the age-old philosophical *problem of evil*, i.e. why and/or how an all-powerful, all-loving God permits evil in His creation. Perhaps you can begin to get a sense of the issues within the early Church surrounding the accurate transmission of the authentic teachings of Jesus and where they could have begun to be misunderstood or distorted.

"Owning" God

Since the earliest days of ancient antiquity, man's unholy pride and desire for superiority and dominance over those who are different have repeatedly affirmed his inherent and unquenchable desire to possess exclusive status with his god(s). This tragic and sinful craving by man to want to exclude others from the love and grace of God seems to be woven into man's very DNA, and is continually fighting to overpower man's more divine potential accruing from his creation in God's image.

The Jews were demonstrably possessed by this desire for exclusivity with their God throughout the Old Testament in spite of His repeatedly telling them *they had been chosen for His purpose*–that all nations and people would be blessed through them – *not for their privilege*. God expresses this divine purpose no less than five times in Genesis alone, as well as other places throughout the Bible. Our desire to "own" God and possess exclusive status with Him is not a flattering reflection on the legacy of our faith or man's earnestness in pursuing the truth about God.

As noted above, evidence suggests this less than benevolent and exclusionary "Christian" perception of God began with a contradictory and conditional declaration of His grace by the Roman Church after the faith had been subsumed by the power and politics of a declining Roman Empire. To put it bluntly, the theocratic marriage of politics and religion make pernicious bedfellows, which is why the founding fathers of the United States were so astute in separating the two.

Conditional Grace

Let's quickly explore why the still orthodox Christian view of (limited) grace established as official Church doctrine by Roman Emperor Justinian in the 6th century AD (more on this later) is contradictory to the notion of grace held by most people.

An online search for the definition of grace turns up the following among numerous definitions.

> *"A capacity to tolerate, accommodate, or forgive people."*
>
> *"In Christianity, the infinite love, mercy, favor, and goodwill shown to humankind by God."*

I believe these definitions correspond with most people's notion of grace, Christian or otherwise, as "unmerited favor". However, the problem is they don't align with the current dominant (i.e. orthodox) Christian doctrine of God's grace as it pertains to non-Christians.

As every person knows, orthodox Christian doctrine holds that God condemns all non-Christians to an eternity of conscious torment in hell for failing to accept Jesus Christ as their personal Lord and Savior prior to their death. To be fair, some Christians make exceptions for infants and children who have not reached the age of majority, mentally incompetent people, those who have never had the opportunity to hear the Gospel, etc. However, in spite of these exceptions, it is hard for most people to reconcile their view of grace as unmerited favor with the historical Christian view (i.e., for the last 1500 years) of God's conditional grace.

Not only is this contradiction both a logical and emotional issue for many people, including many Christians, but there is also much in the Bible and early Christian history to indicate there is good reason to question whether the traditional Christian view represents God's truth and Jesus' message on this all-important matter. This is what the rest of this book explores, perhaps for the first time for many Christians. I sincerely hope you will continue this journey back to the early roots of our faith and a deeper examination of relevant Biblical scriptures.

Are You Saved?

I'll never forget the Sunday sermon by my pastor. He was preaching on the difference between religion and faith. At one point, he talked about when he was a young pastor and recent graduate of a conservative Christian seminary. He related how exasperated he became when well-intended church members and the many conservative Christians he was surrounded by "wore me out" with their incessant inquiries … "Are you saved?" … "Are you saved?" … "Are you saved?"

Though at first I was somewhat surprised by my pastor's admission, after thinking further about it I started to see what he was saying. Part of his message was that religion, a man-made institution, tends to emphasize what we are to believe (i.e. doctrine) and the end result(s) of doing so (e.g. going to heaven). Faith, on the other hand, is a distinctly personal journey of transformation (i.e. salvation) that involves our coming to a deeper understanding and belief in God, and a genuine striving to live in harmony with His will. As opposed to merely focusing on the end result of "going to heaven" (i.e. being "saved" in the lexicon of some Christians), faith probes the broader spiritual implications of the process and nature of salvation.

In the context of orthodox Christian doctrine, being "saved" generally means gaining eternal life by explicitly accepting Jesus Christ as our Savior before we die, thereby gaining entry into God's heavenly kingdom and spending eternity with Him. To some Christians, salvation is substantially focused on going to heaven, with a seemingly lesser focus on the actual personal and spiritual transformation required to truly enter and dwell in the spiritual kingdom of God. This seeming fixation on heaven is succinctly captured in the popular evangelical question, "If you died today, do you know where you would spend eternity?"

In its most extreme manifestation, some Christians appear to be so obsessed with going to heaven that they are eagerly awaiting the violent and apocalyptic return of Jesus as believed to be prophesied in Scripture. Much of Christendom appears to have given up on Jesus saving the world and has concluded the only way for God to save it is to essentially destroy it, as they believe is foretold in the Book of Revelation. More on this later.

As already mentioned, this book is about what I believe is an almost two-millennia-old misunderstanding of what Jesus and the Bible actually have to say, or not, about the conventional Christian doctrine of hell and eternal punishment. However, it is only fair that we ask if perhaps part of this misunderstanding is rooted in another misunderstanding … the currently prevalent Christian notion of what it means to be "saved". If salvation is only about the traditional Christian belief of going to heaven because you have accepted Jesus Christ before you die, then not being saved must mean something which contradicts or is opposite of this notion. Right? Well, perhaps not … for several reasons.

The Kindom of God = The Kingdom of Heaven

First, let's clarify two of the New Testament's key phrases. Virtually all theologians agree that in the New Testament the phrases "kingdom of God" and "kingdom of Heaven" are equivalent. They mean the same thing. I would encourage you to check this out for yourself.

"Kingdom of God" occurs 70 times in the New Testament while "kingdom of Heaven" occurs 33 times, all in the Gospel of Matthew. Theologians believe Matthew was writing for a Jewish audience and since it was forbidden for God's name to be written or spoken, he opted to use the phrase "kingdom of Heaven" in lieu of "kingdom of God". However, it is interesting to note that Matthew also contains four occurrences of the phrase "kingdom of God", used in the context of it being spoken by Jesus himself. Since Matthew presumably understood Jesus to be God, Jesus could clearly say His own name.

The clearest argument that the two phrases mean the same thing is that there are at least four accounts within the Gospels of events in which Matthew uses the kingdom of Heaven and one of the other three Gospel writers, or Matthew himself, uses kingdom of God to describe the same event. Here's the list. Check it out for yourself.

1. Matt 4:17 and Mark 1:15 (the kingdom is near/ at hand)
2. Matt 19:14 and Mark 10:13-16 (the kingdom belongs to children)
3. Matt 13:31 and Mark 4:30-31 (the parable of the mustard seed)
4. Matt 5:3 and Luke 6:20 (the poor receive the kingdom)

OK … the kingdom of God and kingdom of Heaven are one and the same … so what? If that is the case, then "going to heaven" (i.e. the orthodox notion of salvation) is the equivalent of attaining or entering into the kingdom of God. So what do Jesus and the New Testament have to say about attaining/entering into the kingdom of God? This is where it starts to get interesting.

When Jesus speaks of the kingdom of God in the New Testament, he is most often speaking about a spiritual realm that is near and imminent, and capable of being entered into while we are still on this earth. The kingdom of God (i.e. heaven) is breaking into THIS world NOW and is NEAR, he says. It is not just a future time and place attainable only after we die.

In one dramatic exchange with the Pharisees, Jesus explains,

> "The kingdom of God does not come with your careful observation, nor will people say, 'Here it is,' or 'There it is,' because the kingdom of God is within you." (Luke 17:20-21 NIV)

Instead of "within you", some Bible translations say "among you" or "in your midst". Wow … the kingdom of God is within or among us! Who knew? It's probably safe to say that's the first time the Jewish religious authorities had ever heard anything quite like that.

That's not the only place Jesus seems to turn the conventional notion of heaven upside down so to speak … instead of heaven being "up there", it can actually be found "down here" … within and among us! Here are a few examples from the NIV Bible.

- In Matt 3:2, 4:17, 10:7; Mark 1:15; Luke 10:9, 11, 21:31; Jesus says the kingdom of God "is near" or "at hand", depending on translation, on *seven different occasions.*

- In two verses (Matt 12:28 and Luke 11:20) in which Jesus is responding to the Pharisees' accusation that he is driving out demons in the name of Beelzebub (Satan), Jesus says, "But if I drive out demons by the Spirit [finger] of God, *then the kingdom of God has come upon [to] you.*" [Luke wording]

- In another instance, Jesus told one of the teachers of the law, "*You are not far from the kingdom of God.*" (Mark 12:34) when he agreed with Jesus' response to the question, "What is the most important commandment under the law?"

- In Mark 9:1 and Luke 9:27, Jesus tells the crowds to which he is speaking that "some who are standing here *will not taste death before they see the kingdom of God.*"

- In speaking of Joseph of Arimathea, the "good and upright man" who claimed Jesus' body after his crucifixion, both Mark 15:43 and Luke 23:51 described him as "*waiting for the kingdom of God.*"

By entering the following URLs into your Internet browser address bar [or clicking on the links below if you're reading this as an ebook], you can quickly see all the occurrences of the phrases "kingdom of God" and "kingdom of Heaven" in the NIV New Testament.

http://www.biblegateway.com/keyword/?search=kingdom of god&version=NIV&searchtype=phrase

http://www.biblegateway.com/keyword/?search=kingdom of heaven&version=NIV&searchtype=phrase

Upon a comprehensive examination of the context of the 96 New Testament verses referencing the kingdom of God or kingdom of Heaven, it appears that perhaps as many as 40-45 of them are discussing the kingdom of God/Heaven as a present reality, not just a future event or phenomenon. To be fair, there are approximately seven instances in which Jesus refers to the kingdom of God/Heaven in a seemingly future context. However, it is not my contention that the kingdom of God/Heaven is confined to the here and now of this world, but rather that the reign of God's kingdom *began* in this world with the advent of Jesus' ministry and will continue until God is "*all in all*" (1 Cor 15:28). That is, until God has restored His creation and all people to Himself. It is my contention that is the only salvation worthy of, and that will bring ultimate glory to, an omnipotent and perfectly loving God who "*so loved the world, that He gave His only begotten son.*"

Most of the 96 New Testament verses pertaining to the kingdom of God/Heaven are Jesus' words and parables describing: *what the kingdom is like* (Matt 13:24, 31, 33, 44, 45, 47, 52; 18:23; 20:1; 22:2; Mark 4:26, 30; Luke 13:18, 20) or *who does, has or hasn't yet gained entry into the kingdom*, and *how, when and in what order* (Matt 5:3, 10, 19, 20; 11:11; 18:1, 3, 4; 19:14, 23, 24; 21:32; 23:13; Mark 10:14, 15, 23, 24, 25; Luke 6:20; 18:16, 17; John 3:3, 5; Acts 14:22; 1 Cor 6:9, 10; Gal 5:21).

It is clear from virtually all these verses that the kingdom of God/Heaven is a spiritual kingdom, not physical, most easily accessible by the poor, persecuted and downtrodden, and those with child-like faith. Worldly riches and self-righteousness will not help us enter into the promise of God's kingdom, but rather take us further away from truly grasping the absolute faith, trust in, and obedience to God required for admission.

As Jesus himself noted in Matthew when he was chastising the chief priests and elders in the temple,

> *Jesus said to them, "I tell you the truth, the tax collectors and the prostitutes are entering the kingdom of God ahead of you. For John came to you to show you the way of righteousness, and you did not believe him, but the tax collectors and the prostitutes did. And even after you saw this, you did not repent and believe him. (Matt 21:31-32 NIV)*

Perhaps surprising to many people, Jesus did not exclude from God's kingdom even the arrogant, self-righteous Jewish religious leaders to whom his disapproval in the Gospels is almost exclusively directed, though he did claim their entry into the kingdom would be *after* the sinners they so vociferously condemned. And perhaps in the most magnanimous and grace-filled gesture in human history, as he died on the cross Jesus beseeched God to show mercy on those who so wantonly and callously rejected and crucified him,

> *"Father, forgive them, for they do not know what they are doing." (Luke 23:34 NIV)*

Is there any doubt that in his final moments, Jesus was asking God to demonstrate his unconditional love to even those who so blatantly and brutally rejected him, and by extension God? Could this merciful request by Jesus at the pinnacle of his earthly suffering and rejection be any more clear as to his intentions with respect to his Father's kingdom for those who had rejected (or reject) him?

Hopefully, as a result of this brief examination of Scripture, we now understand the kingdom of God/Heaven in this broader spiritual context that does not limit being "saved" or "going to heaven" to simply what happens after we die. In light of this more spiritual understanding, the traditional Christian doctrines of hell and eternal punishment need to be reexamined as well. That's what the remainder of this book is about.

Shall we begin?

The "New" Old Testament

Many Christians believe God's judgment and eternal punishment of sinners is one of the clearest, most dominant themes of the Bible. They believe it begins in the Old Testament and carries through consistently and uniformly throughout the New Testament. Ironically, this view, particularly with respect to the Old Testament, is demonstrably mistaken, and has already been or is being rectified in most modern Bibles.

Contrary to what has been popular Christian opinion, ***there is no notion of post mortem punishment in the Old Testament***, though a few scriptures appear to indicate a reuniting with God following death. Surprised? Let's look at some evidence that this is the case.

The Fate of Old Testament Characters

Let's begin with some simple observations that have been overlooked by many Christians.

In ALL the Old Testament stories – Adam and Eve (Gen 2:4-3:24), Cain and Abel (Gen 4:1-17), Noah and the Flood (Gen 6:1-9:17), Sodom and Gomorrha (Gen 18-19), etc. – there is no mention of anyone being eternally punished or going to hell (or anything remotely resembling orthodox Christianity's conception of hell) for their sins against God. Nor is there any mention or threat of eternal punishment in the Law of Moses, Levitical Law, or any other Old Testament judgments and punishments. To be fair, there are some stories of people being killed (or destroyed) by God for disobeying Him. We will discuss some of these instances later.

So what is the eternal status of the subjects of these Old Testament stories? Ironically, in virtually all cases, the Bible never says in either the Old or New Testaments. However, it is mentioned that Elijah is taken up to heaven, and in Jesus' New Testament *parable* of Lazarus and the rich man, Abraham is implied as being with God in heaven after his death, though there is no mention of Abraham's post mortem fate in the Old Testament. Other than Jesus and a couple of other New Testament figures, these are the few examples of where anything specific, or at all, is said as to the eternal fate of most of the central actors in the Bible.

Given the significance of our eternal destiny to orthodox Christian doctrine, one might expect God to have said more and made it much clearer in His Word as to the fate of these sinners in some of the most central stories of the Old Testament, *particularly since the Old Testament represents almost three-fourths of the verses in the entire Bible and several thousand years of man's history in which God was supposedly actively speaking to His prophets!*

Not only that, but some of these Old Testament characters' sins were pretty serious. After all, according to traditional doctrine, Adam and Eve's violation of God's prohibition to not eat from the Tree of Knowledge of Good and Evil caused the fall of the ENTIRE human race! That's a major wrench they threw into God's plan for His creation. You might think if anyone's transgressions against God warranted eternal punishment, Adam and Eve might be him or her. However, all we know about their fate was that they were cast out of the Garden of Eden and subsequently died at what appear to be relatively ripe old ages. There is no mention of any post-mortem punishment, eternal or otherwise.

Consider Cain who committed the first murder … against his own brother! From Scripture, all we know about God's punishment of Cain is this:

> *When you cultivate the ground, it will no longer yield its strength to you; you will be a vagrant and a wanderer on the earth. (Gen 4:12 NIV)*

But after an appeal from Cain, God's heart seems to soften toward him.

> *So the LORD said to him, "Therefore whoever kills Cain, vengeance will be taken on him sevenfold " And the LORD appointed a sign for Cain, so that no one finding him would slay him. (Gen 4:15 NIV)*

And that's the last we hear of Cain's fate in the Bible. This lack of any eternal destiny for these central characters is the case with virtually all of the other key stories of the Old Testament.

"What about Sodom and Gomorrah?" you might ask. According to this story, Sodom and Gomorrah and their sinful citizens were destroyed (not punished forever) by burning sulfur rained down from heaven by the Lord (Gen 19:24-25). As horrible as their fate might sound, there is a little known redemptive sequel to this story.

The Old Testament book of Ezekiel describes a seldom-acknowledged account of the restoration of Sodom and her "daughters" (i.e. Gomorrah) in which God *himself* makes atonement (Eze 16:53-55 NIV) for their sins as part of one of His recurring episodes of forgiveness of Jerusalem. The relevant verse from that story follows:

> *And your sisters, Sodom with her daughters and Samaria with her daughters, will return to what they were before;*
> *(Eze 16:55 NIV)*

To most Christians, these *facts* about these stories are contrary to what they *think* the Old Testament teaches about God's judgment and punishment. However, it gets even more interesting.

(NO) Hell in the Old Testament

For more than three centuries, the King James Bible, first published in 1611, was the translation used by the vast majority of Protestant denominations within Christendom. This English translation of the Old Testament contained 31 references to "hell". This can be readily confirmed at the Bible search site BibleGateway.com by entering the following URL into your browser address bar.

http://www.biblegateway.com/keyword/?search=hell&version=KJV&-searchtype=phrase

"Sheol" is the Hebrew word in the Old Testament Scriptures translated as "hell" by the King James translators. The only problem is sheol never meant or implied anything remotely similar to the orthodox Christian concept of hell to the Old Testament Jews. In the Hebrew Scriptures, sheol is the word for a grave or death. It applies to all who die, good or bad, and connotes no notion of post-mortem judgment. The Hebrew Scriptures contained no reference to or concept of eternal punishment for one's sins against God, or eternal life for that matter.

Most modern Bible translations have corrected this paradigm-changing translation error. The following sample of well-known Bibles, both contemporary and older, contains **ZERO** occurrences of the word "hell" in the Old Testament. The following URL addresses link to the search for the word "hell" in the Bible version immediately above at the website www.biblegateway.com.

New International Version
http://www.biblegateway.com/keyword/?search=hell&searchtype=phrase&version=NIV

American Standard Version
http://www.biblegateway.com/keyword/?search=hell&searchtype=phrase&version=ASV

New American Standard Version
http://www.biblegateway.com/keyword/?search=hell&searchtype=phrase&version=NASB

English Standard Version
http://www.biblegateway.com/keyword/?search=hell&searchtype=phrase&version=ESV

Amplified Version
http://www.biblegateway.com/keyword/?search=hell&searchtype=phrase&version=AMP

Contemporary English Version
http://www.biblegateway.com/keyword/?search=hell&searchtype=phrase&version=CEV

New Century Version
http://www.biblegateway.com/keyword/?search=hell&searchtype=phrase&version=NCV

Young's Literal Translation
http://www.biblegateway.com/keyword/?search=hell&searchtype=phrase&version=YLT

Darby Translation
http://www.biblegateway.com/keyword/?search=hell&searchtype=phrase&version=DARBY

How could it have taken 300 years to correct this spectacular error in the King James Bible? Not only that, but for how many centuries before the King James translations did Christians erroneously believe this is what the Old Testament taught? As we will see, the answer to the latter question is approximately 1200 years, or from the time of the creation of the first Latin Bible at the end of the 4th century AD. So, for at least 1500 years, Christians labored under a complete misrepresentation of what the original Hebrew Scriptures said on this all-important matter. To put it more acutely: *That was 1500 years of verifiably wrong teaching that the Old Testament attested to the existence of hell.* Sadly, as we will see, this was not the only significant translation error that occurred relative to the Church doctrine of hell and eternal punishment.

The entire tone and understanding of the Old Testament is forever altered by the removal of hell from the 31 verses that were previously thought to have taught it. This new lens for understanding the Hebrew Scriptures has a profound effect on the image of God described there, particularly when considered in conjunction with Old Testament Scriptures that present a more merciful picture of God that have been difficult for many people to reconcile with the hell Scriptures.

A Loving, Benevolent God

There are many Old Testament passages and Psalms that describe a merciful God who is "longsuffering" (i.e. patient) and will not allow His children to die in sin and separation from Him. Here are a few verses that portray this very different picture of God's love, mercy, forgiveness and grace. Some of them specifically contradict the subsequent Christian hell-notion of a God that would punish some of His children forever.

..., so we must die. But God does not take away life; instead, he devises ways so that a banished person may not remain estranged from him. (2 Sam 14:14 NIV)

The LORD is compassionate and gracious, slow to anger, abounding in love. He will not always accuse, nor will he harbor his anger forever; (Ps 103:8-9 NIV)

'I, even I, am he who blots out your transgressions, for my own sake, and remembers your sins no more.' (Isa 43:25 NIV)

he [God] says: 'It is too small a thing for you to be my servant to restore the tribes of Jacob and bring back those of Israel I have kept. I will also make you a light for the Gentiles, that you may bring my salvation to the ends of the earth.' (Isa 49:6 NIV)

and the dust returns to the ground it came from, and the spirit returns to God who gave it. (Ecc 12:7 NIV)

O you who hear prayer, to you all people will come. (Ps 65:2 NIV)

'I will punish their sin ... but I will not take my love from him, nor will I ever betray my faithfulness.' (Ps 89:32-33 NIV)

For the LORD is good and his love endures forever. (Ps 100:5 NIV) ["his love endures forever" occurs 41 times in the NIV OT]

Praise the LORD, O my soul, ... who forgives all your sins and ... who redeems your life from the pit [sheol] and crowns you with love and compassion, (Ps 103:2-4 NIV)

> *... he [God] will destroy the shroud that enfolds all peoples, the sheet that covers all nations; he will swallow up death [sheol] forever. (Isa 25:7-8 NIV)*

In light of these benevolent views of God's unconditional love and grace and the *factual* re-interpretation of original Scriptures due to the mistranslation of sheol, it would seem all Christians should feel compelled to seek out a deeper understanding of our *current* Bible translations' truth about God.

Perhaps another more recent example will provide further impetus for our reassessment of Scripture. In the New International Version Bible (first published in 1973 and updated in 1984 by the International Bible Society) there are two verses in the Old Testament that appear to refer to the eternal destruction of a person (the other "eternal" fate of sinners thought to be mentioned in the Bible). One of these is in Proverbs.

> *A false witness will perish, and whoever listens to him will be destroyed forever. (Prov 21:28 NIV)*

Perhaps it's just me, but that seems like a pretty severe fate for listening to a false witness. Interestingly, the NIV is the only Bible translation that alludes to this harsh fate in this particular verse. Here are a few of the other translations of this same verse.

New King James Version (NKJV)	A false witness shall perish, But the man who hears him will speak endlessly.
New American Standard Bible (NASB)	A false witness will perish, But the man who listens to the truth will speak forever.
English Standard Version (ESV)	A false witness will perish but the word of a man who hears will endure.
Young's Literal Translation (YLT)	A false witness doth perish, And an attentive man for ever speaketh.

As you can see, not only do these translations not agree with the 1984 NIV, some of them contain different meanings even among themselves. However, the further mystery to the NIV translation of Proverbs 21:28 is that the latest version of the New International Version [published in 2011 by the same International Bible Society] has dramatically altered its language and meaning as follows:

> *Those who give false witness will perish, but a careful listener will testify successfully. (Prov 21:28 TNIV)*

Why, after almost 40 years, did the NIV translators finally decide they had gotten the translation of Proverbs 21:28 wrong? What does this say about how certain we should be of other controversial verses and contested words in the Bible?

Though each person must come to their own answers on these puzzling questions, the fact remains that Bible translations are not static, nor in full agreement with other translations. Significant changes in scriptural understanding, and perhaps the very nature and purpose of God, can occur when words or verses are re-interpreted with new or different meanings. Even the conservative Christian Apologetics Research Ministry (CARM) acknowledges the copies of original Scriptures that comprise our modern Bibles are NOT inspired.

> *"The doctrine of the inspiration of the Bible means that the Bible in the original documents is God-breathed, that it is a divine product ... The copies of those documents are not inspired. We have copies of inspired documents." (http://www.carm.org/bible/inspiration.htm)*

What CARM fails to mention is that many of these copies are not in total agreement among themselves, and different Bible translations are not in agreement on some critical translation issues.

"Forever" in the Old Testament

There is another Hebrew word in the Old Testament Scriptures that needs to be mentioned at this point. The Hebrew word "olam" has traditionally been interpreted as meaning eternal or forever, and still has this interpretation in many Bibles. Most Hebrew and Old Testament scholars insist olam never denoted the idea of eternity, endless time, or "forever". It merely represented the notion of an unknown or "hidden" period of time.

Young's Literal Translation Bible (YLT, 1898), which we will talk more about later, translates olam as "age-during", the 19th century way of saying "lasting for an age". There are many events described in the Hebrew Scriptures as "olam" which had a finite but unknown duration or timeframe (e.g. Jonah's time in the whale's belly, the Aaronic priesthood, the earthly rule of the line of King David, Solomon's kingship, the duration of the 2nd temple, etc.).

It is agreed by virtually all Hebrew and Old Testament scholars that neither the Old Testament Jews nor the Jews of Christ's time had any notion of eternity or time without end. The Jews thought in terms of successive ages of time, each having an uncertain or unknown end date (i.e. "age-during" in the YLT). This will be important to our discussion of one of the key mistranslated words of the New Testament.

Another independent perspective on the development of the idea of eternity is found at the Stanford Encyclopedia of Philosophy (http://plato.stanford.edu/entries/eternity/, December 2013).

> *"Concepts of eternity have developed in a way that is, as a matter of fact, closely connected to the development of the concept of God in Western thought, beginning with ancient Greek philosophers; particularly to the idea of God's relation to time, the idea of divine perfection, and the Creator-creature distinction. Eternity as timelessness, and eternity as everlastingness, have been distinguished. Following the work of Boethius and Augustine of Hippo divine timelessness became the dominant view. In more recent times, those who stress a more anthropomorphic account of God, or God's immanence within human history, have favored divine everlastingness."*

"Divine timelessness" (i.e. God exists outside of time) did not become the "dominant view" until the time of Boethius and Augustine *approximately four hundred years after Jesus lived.* The concept of "divine everlastingness" (i.e. eternity) appears to have emerged even later. Given that, it raises a serious question as to whether the idea of eternal punishment *by God* could have been the dominant view at the time of Jesus and during the first century AD when the New Testament was written. As we have already seen, it's certainly not found in the Old Testament.

The even more interesting question we will explore further in later chapters is: When and on what basis did the doctrine of eternal punishment become the orthodox doctrine of the Christian Church?

Inconsistent Images of God

One other item worth briefly discussing is what many Christians consider to be inconsistent images of God presented in the Old Testament. It is distinctly possible that some of the harsher, discordant images of God were contributors to the conditional view of God's love and grace that was ultimately adopted by orthodox Christianity. Let me explain.

The Cleansing of Canaan

According to the Old Testament, God is described as having instructed the Jews to totally cleanse Canaan, the Promised Land, of all pagan tribes.

> *However, in the cities of the nations the LORD your God is giving you as an inheritance, do not leave alive anything that breathes. Completely destroy them — the Hittites, Amorites, Canaanites, Perizzites, Hivites and Jebusites–as the LORD your God has commanded you. (Deuteronomy 20:16-17)*

The traditional Christian explanation of God's command is that all non-believers had to be eliminated from God's holy land to prevent the Jews from being corrupted by pagan influences through intermarriage or other means.

A specific example of the Jews' efforts to carry out God's assumed command is found in Joshua, though there are others in the Old Testament as well.

> *So Joshua subdued the whole region, ... He left no survivors. He totally destroyed all who breathed, just as the LORD, the God of Israel, had commanded. (Joshua 10:40)*

According to this verse, Joshua was commanded by God to kill every man, woman and child in this area, as well as the rest, of Canaan.

Of course, most Christians know that the Jews failed to carry out God's instructions. They did not cleanse the entire Promised Land and the pagan peoples living among them frequently corrupted them by enticing them back into worshipping idols and following pagan practices.

Many people, Christians and non-Christians alike, struggle with God commanding the Jews to kill the occupants of the Promised Land. In addition to the potential contradictions in God's moral character presented by these Old Testament verses, another often-overlooked issue is their illogical inconsistency with one of God's core attributes – His omniscience.

The Omniscience Conundrum

According to orthodox Christian doctrine, God knows all things past, present and future. The theological term used to describe this aspect of God is omniscience. Can you see the problem beginning to develop with respect to God's moral character based on His command to cleanse the Promised Land and the Jews' failure to do so? **If God is omniscient, He knew the Jews would fail to carry out His command to cleanse the Promised Land even before He issued it!**

Given that is true, what does this imply about Joshua's killing of so many Gentiles in Canaan? One might reasonably contend it was pointless, and potentially ethnic cleansing commanded by God, as opposed to the conventional Christian explanation of its being God's "justice" carried out on non-believers.

Another Understanding?

To say the least, the above picture of God is disturbing to many Christians and non-Christians. I submit it has in fact contributed to many people discounting God, or Christianity as a legitimate worldview of God's ultimate nature, purpose and plan. But could there be another understanding of these verses?

Could these Old Testament accounts illustrate the problems and dangers inherent in believing any person or group possesses exclusive status with God or understanding of His will? Perhaps Joshua and Moses did not fully grasp God's will regarding the means by which the Jew's were to occupy or govern the Promised Land. Perhaps Joshua projected his own harsh disposition toward pagan tribes onto his belief about what God was instructing him to do. He would not be the first or last person to do that. How many Christians have been guilty of this very thing throughout history? Don't the Inquisition, slavery, and the denial of civil rights to African-Americans represent Exhibit A for Christians misreading the Bible … and misunderstanding God?

Orthodox Christianity also maintains this happened with the Jews of Jesus' time. Throughout history, Christians have contended they were obsessed with the Law and missed the Messiah. Given that is the case, when did the Jews first begin to make these errors in understanding God's will? Is it so hard to believe it may have happened throughout Jewish history? In fact, aren't the Old Testament Jewish prophets themselves testimony that it did? Isn't this the human condition since the beginning of time?

All Christians should seriously consider the possibility there may be alternative understandings of the traditional interpretations of those Biblical accounts that do not easily reconcile with our consciences, which must surely come from the very image of God within us. Many injustices and atrocities throughout history could have been averted if we had.

Zapping Uzzah

I offer one other Old Testament story that is confusing to many committed Christians. This is the story of Uzzah in 2 Samuel.

> *David and the whole house of Israel were celebrating with all their might before the LORD, … Uzzah reached out and took hold of the ark of God, because the oxen stumbled. The LORD's anger burned against Uzzah because of his irreverent act; therefore God struck him down and he died there beside the ark of God. (2 Sam 6:5-7)*

Wow! That's a serious punishment for what one might reasonably argue was an innocent act to prevent something *even more irreverent* from happening to the ark of God … letting it fall off the cart to the ground. Surely God, does not violate His own commandment … Thou shalt not kill … for something as seemingly innocent and well intended as Uzzah's attempt to keep the ark of God from falling to the ground, even if David and Uzzah were being careless (or irreverent) in transporting the Ark. Given their mutual carelessness/irreverence, we might also ask why David was not also struck down?

I don't think it's unreasonable to question how one can confidently believe in and worship a seemingly capricious god like the one depicted in this account. The traditional Christian explanation that God is sovereign and just, so whatever He does to punish sin is by definition just, does not ring true to many sincere seekers of the truth.

For many Christians, these issues present genuine and serious questions regarding the image of God taught by orthodox Christian doctrine. Simply asserting God is just or fair in His judgment and punishment of sinners or non-believers in light of these questions does not satisfy the moral compass of more than a few people. Perceived inconsistencies in Scripture, as well as recent changes in many English Bibles' translations of Hebrew words like sheol and verses like Proverbs 21:28, only magnify the questions these Christians have about the proper role and understanding of Scripture, and ultimately the truth about God's nature, purpose and will.

Between the Old and New Testaments

Most Bible scholars believe the Old Testament was completed sometime between 500-200 BC. It is also almost universally agreed among Old Testament scholars that up to that time the Jews had no developed notion of an afterlife and, as we have already shown, no notion of post mortem punishment for sin. However, the Jewish notion of death being the ultimate human end began to change after the Jewish nation was repeatedly defeated and overrun by successive foreign enemies and their accompanying civilizations, and exposed to their pagan religious beliefs.

This process of being defeated and occupied by enemies repeated itself throughout Jewish history as told in the Old Testament and began for the final time around 722 BC when the Assyrians defeated Israel, the northern Jewish kingdom. The progression began to accelerate when the southern Jewish kingdom, Judah, fell around 587 BC to the Babylonians, who had conquered the Assyrians some 25 years before. The fall of Israel and Judah caused the displacement and disintegration of the twelve tribes of Israel and their assimilation into the cultures of their pagan conquerors, leading to what are now called the Lost Tribes of Israel.

The Occupation of the Jews

From this time forward the Jews lived under serial subjugation by various pagan nations for the next approximately 800 years until the Jewish nation ceased to exist after the destruction of the 2nd Temple by the Romans in 67 AD. In succession, these foreign occupiers were Assyria, Babylonia, Persia, Greece, the Hellenized Ptolemaic (Egyptian) and Seleucid (Syrian) kingdoms, and finally the Romans. The only exception to this was the roughly 100-year independent Maccabean period that began around 165 BC and ended around 67 BC with the fall of the region to the Roman Empire.

Suffice it to say the Jews were exposed to and became well acquainted with the pantheon of gods of the various religions associated with each of these foreign nations and cultures, and the belief in an afterlife that was common to all of them. Toward the end of this long period of serial occupation, Jewish apocryphal (and apocalyptic) literature began to refer to life after death with rewards for good people (typically Jews) and punishments for sinners (typically their Gentile conquerors). However, as the concept of eternity had not likely evolved by that time, as previously discussed, this punishment appears to have been temporal in nature and commensurate with the misdeeds of the person believed to be due for punishment.

Though some orthodox Christian authorities would perhaps contest this assertion of the temporal nature of the Jews' pre-Christian belief in punishment in the afterlife, we will explain how the orthodox view of an eternal aspect to this punishment is the result of a faulty translation and interpretation of several key Greek words – hades, gehenna, tartarus, aion and aionios.

Hell Facts in the New Testament

We have now come to where "the rubber meets the road" … so to speak. Quite naturally since we're discussing the origins of the Christian doctrines of hell and eternal punishment, what Jesus and the New Testament have to say about these critical concepts is of utmost importance. Unfortunately, ascertaining what he and the New Testament authors might have actually said is not as simple as picking up your favorite Bible translation and just reading what it says they said. Just as with the King James Old Testament translation errors of the original Hebrew scriptures, many current Bibles *presently* contain similar translation errors of key New Testament Greek words that have popularly and erroneously been understood to represent hell and eternal punishment. To begin to appreciate where these translations went wrong, we need to better understand:

- the transition from the Greek/Hellenistic influence and language of the Holy Lands shortly before Christ to the domination of the Jews and early Christians

by the Roman Empire in the first five centuries following the life of Jesus; and

- the ultimate adoption of and influence upon what became Christianity by the Romans and the associated transition from the Koine Greek language of the New Testament to the Latin upon which the first Bible, the Latin Vulgate, was based.

Our goal is to trace this history and transition over the course of the first quarter of the Christian era to better understand the indelible Roman influence on the Christian doctrines of hell and eternal punishment believed by many, if not most, Christians today. Our task is something akin to a forensic investigation of the evolution of a few critical words as they were translated from the original Hebrew and Koine Greek into the Latin language of what became the first official Church Bible, the Latin Vulgate. Let's get started.

What Jesus Had to Say About Hell

One Sunday morning the pastor of a church my wife and I attended while visiting another city made the statement, during his sermon on the Luke 16 parable of Lazarus and the rich man, that Jesus spoke more about hell in the Gospels than he did about heaven! This was not the first time I had heard this particular sentiment from various Christian ministers, and I do not doubt they sincerely believe this is what the Bible might say.

However, having said that, I do have a few questions as to their beliefs on this particular issue.

1. Did they come to this view as a result of their own study and research of Biblical translation and/or interpretation, or was this the understanding taught to them at the particular seminary or Bible College they attended?
2. How much time have they personally spent seriously investigating the historical and exegetical roots of this

exclusive Christian view which has come to symbolize Christianity to much of the non-Christian world?

3. If compelling evidence were presented that this is NOT what the Gospels or the rest of the New Testament really teach, would they be open to reconsider their view on this arguably most contentious and disputed tradition in all of Christendom?

I would hope all people would be open to listening to the history and facts surrounding this vital issue. In the Gospel of John, Jesus tells us,

> *If you hold to my teaching, you are really my disciples. Then you will know the truth, and the truth will set you free. (John 8:31-32)*

As we will see, what the original New Testament Scriptures and Jesus actually said about hell, when properly translated and interpreted, differs significantly from what traditional Christianity has historically taught, and most Christians have believed or assumed. Let's begin with the alleged references to hell in our English Bibles.

Three Words ... One Meaning?

In various English versions of the New Testament, the word "hell" is *inconsistently* translated from three different Greek words. These three words are (in order of frequency in the original Greek)–gehenna (12 occurrences), hades (11 occurrences) and tartarus (1 occurrence). In the original Greek Gospels, Jesus only uses the words gehenna (11 occurrences) and hades (4 occurrences) according to Young's Literal Translation Bible that is arguably viewed to be the most accurate translation of scripture. More on this later.

Clearly if three Greek words have variously been translated to our English word and concept for hell, then one might naturally conclude the three words all roughly mean the same thing. It is not uncommon in many modern languages to have different words with the same or similar meanings. We call them synonyms. Generally however, there are differences, often subtle, in the precise connotation of each of the similar words. One might presume this would be the case with more limited ancient languages like Koine Greek, the original language of the New Testament.

Irrespective of how any particular Bible might have translated these words, the specific question that must be considered is: Did these three Greek words – gehenna, hades and tartarus– all refer to a place of eternal punishment at the time the New Testament authors wrote the Gospel?

[A quick note: Notice I did not include the words Jesus might have actually used in the above question. Jesus spoke Aramaic, a derivative language from the ancient Hebrew of the original Jewish Scriptures and the common language of Galilee, Jesus' home area. However, the Gospels record Jesus' words in the more broadly understood Koine Greek of the time, with one or two exceptions in which Jesus' actual Aramaic word(s) were used. But specifically in the verses allegedly pertaining to hell, we do not have a record of the Aramaic words Jesus may have spoken.]

Keeping the key question above in mind, let's investigate each of these words.

Gehenna – Origin and Usage

The origin of the Greek word gehenna is from the Old Testament Hebrew "ge Hinnom", meaning the "valley of Hinnom". This was an actual valley located southeast and just outside of Jerusalem. It is mentioned 13 times in 11 different verses in

the Old Testament as "valley of Hinnom," "valley of Ben Hinnom", "valley of the son of Hinnom", or "valley of the children
of Hinnom", depending on the specific Bible translation you
use. It would appear that it was a valley owned or occupied by
a family or tribe called Hinnom for a lengthy period of time
before or during the Old Testament era, though that is just
speculation at this point.

In the later history of the independent Jewish nation
(roughly around 700 BC), the valley of Hinnom became
a place of despicable acts perpetrated by evil and idolatrous
Jewish kings. These desecrations ranged from the sacrifice of
children to Moloch (the idol-god of the Amorites) during the
reign of the apostate Jewish Kings Ahaz and Manasseh, to a
place of child abandonment, to the disposal of human bodies
and Jerusalem garbage in continually burning fires. It also became the place where the bodies of Jewish violators of the Law
were discarded following pronouncement of their guilt and
execution. Given this sordid history, it's not hard to see how
the valley of Hinnom might have come to symbolize a hor-
rific place of judgment and punishment. However, these were
earthly judgments and punishments at the hands of Jewish
kings, judges and religious authorities, not divine punishment
after death by the Lord.

The question we must answer is the following: Did gehenna
subsequently come to represent the place of divine punishment
of sinners after death (i.e. hell) as contended by Christian tradition, and if so was this punishment viewed as eternal?

When the Septuagint was translated from the Jewish Scriptures into Greek sometime during the period 300-100 BC,
gehenna was *ONLY* used to refer to the actual valley of Hinnom. It was not used in any other context. Given this fact, we
can conclude that at that time, roughly 100-300 years before
Jesus, gehenna did not mean hell as we understand it today. So

if gehenna came to stand for the Christian concept of hell by the time of Jesus, it must have happened during the period 300-0 BC, after the Jews had already been living under pagan occupation and influence for at least 300-400 years. By the time Jesus lived, this 600-700 years of pagan influence included exposure to the pagan concept of judgment in an afterlife with rewards and punishments found in the national religions of ALL their foreign occupiers. This means that the orthodox Christian belief in heaven and hell is little to no different than the pagan religions that preceded the birth of Christianity. Are we really comfortable with that?

Beginning in the mid-4th century BC and continuing beyond the time of Jesus, the Greeks and Romans exposed the Jews to a system of multiple gods and other pagan beliefs. In the books of the Apocrypha, we begin to see the influence of the similar Greek and Roman pagan religious systems on the Jewish faith regarding the hope for an afterlife, including reward and punishment language that carried over into the subsequent Latin translation of the Christian Scriptures, but not actually contained or implied in the original Hebrew and Greek scriptures themselves.

The Apocrypha were the quasi-scriptural Hebrew texts authored during the final 200-300 year span of the Jews' Greek and Roman occupation before Jesus. The Jews' lamentation of their plight as subjects and condemnation of their occupiers are key themes in the Apocrypha, and establish the context in which the concept of rewards and punishment after death first begin to appear within Jewish culture and literature. It is not hard to understand how the Jews' accumulating resentment at the 600-700 years of subjugation by their pagan captors might have fueled the adoption of their overlord's beliefs in divine judgment after death, with rewards for virtuous Jews and punishment for their pagan enemies and breakers of the Law. It was also no coincidence their Scripture's prophecy of a messiah who would defeat and punish their enemies gained popular currency at this time as a fervent and broadly held hope for escaping their pagan captors.

It is important to note. In spite of this pre-Jesus emergence of Jewish hope for rewards and punishment after death, there is no evidence either in the Apocrypha or the few other available Jewish writings from before or around this time, including those of Josephus' (the Jewish Pharisee) and Philo of Alexandria (a Jewish Greek philosopher), that indicate the Jews believed gehenna to be a place of divine eternal punishment.

Josephus specifically discussed that the Jews of Jesus' time believed in punishment after death but never used the word gehenna to denote the place or that the punishment was eternal. Philo also never used gehenna to describe the place of punishment after death. Since he was both a Jew and Greek philosopher who published works that fused Jewish faith with Greek philosophy, both of which by then proscribed divine rewards or punishment after death, surely he would have used gehenna to describe this belief if in fact it was either the Greek translation of or the Hebrew word that represented the divine place or eternal nature of this punishment.

The first recorded Christian uses of gehenna to convey the idea of punishment after death (other than those we are questioning in the Bible) was during the period 150-195 AD by Justin Martyr (Italy) and Clement of Alexandria (Egypt). The "fly in the ointment" here is that these men held very different views of the duration of this punishment. Martyr is alleged to believe punishment after death was unending (or eternal), even though it is highly suspect as to whether or not the notion of eternity had even developed by that point in time. Clement believed Jesus and the Gospels taught that God's ultimate plan is to reconcile all of His creation and all people to Himself, and that any punishment after death is temporary and restorative. It appears gehenna did not mean the same thing to both men.

The first documented Jewish usage of gehenna in the context of punishment after death is found in the 3rd century Jewish Targum of Jonathan Ben Uzziel. However, it was used in a temporal sense. This temporary nature of punishment after death is consistent with the dominant body of Jewish belief that persists even to this day.

In further support of this temporal view of gehenna, the following is an excerpt from a discussion of Jewish eschatology at http://en.wikipedia.org/wiki/Jewish_eschatology.

> *"Gehinom is fairly well defined in rabbinic litera-
> ture. It is sometimes translated as "hell", but is much
> closer to the Catholic view of purgatory than to the
> Christian view of hell, which differs from the clas-
> sical Jewish view. Rabbinic thought maintains that
> souls are not tortured in gehinom forever; the longest
> that one can be there is said to be eleven months,
> with the exception of heretics, and unobservant Jews.
> This is the reason that even when in mourning for
> near relatives, Jews will not recite mourner's kaddish
> for longer than an eleven-month period. Gehinom
> is considered a spiritual forge where the soul is puri-
> fied for its eventual ascent to Gan Eden ("Garden of
> Eden")."*

It is helpful to remember that Jesus was a Jew and there is no indication he held any other view of gehenna (i.e. "Gehinom" in Jewish literature) than was held by the Jewish population at the time.

In summary, at the time of Jesus, gehenna had become a place of disposal where things were continually decaying and burning outside the city of Jerusalem. Sound familiar? ... *"Where their worm dieth not, and the fire is not quenched.* [Mark 9:46 KJV] It also may have become a metaphor among the Jews for a place of judgment and punishment for the wicked. But there is no corroborating historical evidence, apart from its *later alleged meaning* in the Bible, that it was thought to represent a place of eternal punishment after death, as does our hell today.

So what exactly does the Bible say about hell?

Hell and Gehenna in the New Testament

Using the popular New International Version (NIV) as a baseline, the following table gives the specific verses in which the words hell and gehenna occur in a few key Bible translations – the King James Version (KJV), the New American Standard Bible (NASB), Young's Literal Translation (YLT), and the Latin Vulgate Bible (LVB). Clearly the Latin Vulgate Bible is not an English Bible, but it will demonstrate a very key point.

Verse	NIV	KJV	NASB	YLT	LVB
Matt 5:22	hell	hell	hell	gehenna	gehennae
Matt 5:29	hell	hell	hell	gehenna	gehennam
Matt 5:30	hell	hell	hell	gehenna	gehennam
Matt 10:28	hell	hell	hell	gehenna	gehennam
Matt 18:9	hell	hell	hell	gehenna	gehennam
Matt 23:15	hell	hell	hell	gehenna	gehennae
Matt 23:33	hell	hell	hell	gehenna	gehennae
Mark 9:43	hell	hell	hell	gehenna	gehennam
Mark 9:45	hell	hell	hell	gehenna	gehennam
Mark 9:47	hell	hell	hell	gehenna	gehennam
Luke 12:5	hell	hell	hell	gehenna	gehennam
James 3:6	hell	hell	hell	gehenna	gehenna
2 Peter 2:4	hell	hell	hell	Tartarus	tartarum

[NOTE: A quick word about Young's Literal Translation. Robert Young, the translator of this Bible version, also compiled the popular and widely used Young's Analytical Concordance. The online Bible resource and search site www.biblegateway.com describes Young's Literal Translation as "an extremely literal translation that attempts to preserve the tense and word usage as found in the original Greek and Hebrew writings."]

There are several interesting observations to be made about the implications of the above verse translations.

First, there is no doubt many modern Bible translators believe that, at the time Jesus lived and the New Testament was originally written (0-100 AD), gehenna represented the notion of hell that has been promulgated by the institutional Church since approximately 500-600 AD. However, it is interesting to note that when the New Testament was translated from Greek to Latin in the late 4th century AD, the Greek word gehenna appears to have been adopted as a new word in the Latin language by the Roman authors as demonstrated by the virtually identical transliteration of the Greek word gehenna to the Latin word forms gehennae/gehennam. This is interesting because the Romans had long before adopted the Greek pantheon of gods (with some differences in names) and the same belief in the afterlife with rewards and punishments, but in hades or tartarus, NOT gehenna. This adoption of gehenna virtually wholesale into the Latin language would be quite natural for a unique *geographic place*, but not for a post-mortem *spiritual place* of punishment that had an already existing parallel within the pre-Christian religious systems of both the Greeks and Romans, and pre-existing words to describe this place–*tartarus* in Greek and *infernum* in Latin.

Next, it is somewhat puzzling that Jesus is not recorded as ever having used the word gehenna in the Gospel of John, arguably the favorite Gospel of more conservative Christians. Nor does John use the word himself in any of his three epistles or in the Book of Revelation, the other New Testament books he is believed to have authored. Many Christians believe Revelation teaches the clearest message and images of hell in the Bible. If gehenna clearly denoted the place of divine eternal punishment at the time John wrote these sacred books, how do we explain these conspicuous omissions?

In addition to John, there is no occurrence of gehenna in the book of Acts, which chronicles the earliest development and sermons of the Church in the first Christian century. If hell was a fundamental doctrine and gehenna was the Greek word representing it, how do we explain it not being used in any context in this central book of the New Testament? It gets even more interesting.

Paul is generally acknowledged as the greatest apostle in first century Christianity. It is a core Christian belief that Paul faithfully taught God's complete truth as miraculously revealed to him by Christ following his crucifixion and resurrection. If that is true, one might naturally think hell would be mentioned in at least one of Paul's thirteen epistles, which comprise almost half of the 27 books of the New Testament. However, it is noticeably absent from ALL of them; it does not occur a single time. If hell was a core Christian doctrine in the early church and Paul was its premier apostle, how do we explain this? It would seem there are only two possibilities—either Paul did not hear or *"faithfully proclaim ... the whole will of God"* (Acts 20:27 NIV), which I'm sure virtually all Christians would strenuously deny, or perhaps Jesus' truth about God has been misconstrued somewhere along the way. Is there any other plausible explanation for this stunning omission by Paul? I can't think of any.

Lastly, I would encourage you to go back and read each of the above twelve verses in which the word hell has been translated from gehenna in Young's Literal Translation Bible (www.

biblegateway.com is an excellent place to do this). To determine these look at the YLT column in the above table, which shows all the occurrences of gehenna in the New Testament. As you read the word gehenna in these verses, think in terms of the historical valley of Hinnom in which despicable atrocities and punishments were committed over the course of Jewish history, and every type of unclean waste (human or otherwise) was constantly being consumed by fire and decay. This valley ultimately represented both a symbol for and physical place of judgment and punishment. Given its very real world existence, how could it possibly have also come to mean a place of post mortem eternal punishment by the time of Jesus?

There is nothing explicit in ANY of the Gospel verses containing gehenna that implies Jesus spoke of it as a place of divine eternal punishment after death. Even in the two verses (Matt 18:9 and Mark 9:47 in some translations) that contrast "life" and the "kingdom of God" with gehenna, we must recall that Jesus *frequently* referred to the kingdom (or reign) of God and kingdom of Heaven as being "near" or "at hand" (depending on translation), and pointedly said "the kingdom of God is within you" (Luke 17:21 NIV). At the time of Jesus, there is little doubt gehenna *symbolized* punishment, death and destruction as opposed to abundant life in God's spiritual kingdom ... in the present, on this earth and within us. But where is the evidence, other than tradition, that it had come to represent a place of divine eternal punishment after death?

Many Bible scholars today are coming to the view that Jesus' *primary message* was not simply a message about escaping this world to a future heavenly kingdom. It is a transformative, personal message about striving to live in and fully reflect God's love and grace in His spiritual kingdom that began breaking into the world with the appearance of Jesus, and which continues and will continue until "every knee shall bow" and "every tongue shall confess to God" (Rom 14:11 KJV). Perhaps Jesus said it best when he prayed, "Thy kingdom come, Thy will be done in earth, as it is in heaven." (Matt 6:10 KJV)

Hades – Origin and Usage

Let's now discuss the historical origins and meaning of the Greek word *hades* within the Greek and Roman religious systems.

Within the Greek pantheon of gods and religious beliefs, "Hades" represented the Greek god of the underworld, and "hades" was the name used for the underworld itself. Hades meant "the hidden one". This underworld (hades) had the same essential meaning to the Greeks as the Hebrew word sheol did to the Old Testament Jews. It was simply the unseen realm where all people, both good and bad, went after death.

In the Greek system of belief, there ultimately developed a concept of judgment for the life one lived. Good people went from hades to Elysium, or the Elysian Fields (roughly corresponding to heaven within orthodox Christianity), and bad people went to tartarus (see the following section), which was ruled by the Greek god Tartarus (or Tartarizo).

The key point here is that, in the Greek language, hades never stood for anything resembling the orthodox Christian concept of hell.

This is illustrated by the fact that in the Greek Septuagint the Hebrew word sheol (meaning either grave or death, depending on the context, and possessing no connotation of post-mortem punishment) is *uniformly* translated as hades. Based upon my research and to the best of my knowledge, no Greek scholar has ever asserted that hades came to represent a place of punishment after death in either the classical or Koine Greek languages. In light of this, one must wonder how and when hades might have come to represent the concept of hell in orthodox Christianity? As we will see, this appears to have occurred when the Greek New Testament was translated into Latin, some 400 years after Jesus' death.

In many English Bible translations, particularly those published since the end of the 19th century, the Greek word hades is most often NOT translated as hell at all, but is simply left as hades or translated to other English words that have nothing to do with hell. The actual translation is highly dependent on which Bible version you are talking about. One has to wonder why this is the case if hades unquestionably referred to hell.

I must also point out that in the Roman pantheon of pagan gods, many of which were adopted directly from the Greeks, the god of the underworld was called Pluto, not Hades, because the later Greeks had begun to refer to Hades as Plouton. However, the Roman poets associated Pluto with the Greek god Tartarus, the god of the lower world where evil people were punished following death. Consequently, the Roman underworld, hades, likewise became associated with the Greek place of punishment after death, tartarus, and was referred to as inferus or infernum, from which the Christian notion of hellfire (inferno) was derived. This appears to have been the genesis of the malevolent interpretation of hades by the early Roman Church. *It is important to note that it came not from the original Greek Christian scriptures, but from pre-Christian Roman pagan traditions via Greek pagan traditions.*

Hell and Hades in the New Testament

Using Young's Literal Translation as the baseline for the occurrences of hades in the original Greek New Testament, the other columns show how hades was translated in the other translations we are analyzing.

Verse	YLT	KJV	NIV	NASB	LVB
Matt 11:23	hades	hell	Hades	Hades	infernum
Matt 16:18	Hades	hell	Hades	Hades	inferi
Luke 10:15	hades	hell	Hades	Hades	infernum
Luke 16:23	hades	hell	Hades	Hades	inferno
Acts 2:27	hades	hell	realm of the dead	Hades	inferno
Acts 2:31	hades	hell	realm of the dead	Hades	inferno
1 Cor 15:55	Hades	grave	death	death	mors
Rev 1:18	hades	hell	Hades	Hades	inferni
Rev 6:8	Hades	Hell	Hades	Hades	inferus
Rev 20:13	hades	hell	Hades	Hades	inferus
Rev 20:14	hades	hell	Hades	Hades	inferus

Like gehenna, there are several interesting observations to make about the translation of hades in the various English New Testaments. Before we mention these, let me also point out that different translations use differing capitalization conventions, making it difficult to ascertain if the word may be referring to Hades (the Greek god) or hades (the Greek realm of the dead).

First, notice the King James Version translates hades as "hell" in all cases except one, 1 Cor 15:55. Both the Latin Vulgate and English Bible translators seem to agree hades meant "death" in that verse. The KJV and Latin Vulgate Bible consistently translate hades to mean the traditional concept of hell, and are noticeably different from the other more modern translations we are examining. It is worth keeping in mind the Latin Vulgate and KJV were the universal translations used by most Christians for more than 1500 (Catholic era) and 400 (Protestant era) years respectively. It is inconceivable to consider any other possibility than that these translations were fundamental to the reinforcement and propagation of the Church's doctrine of hell and eternal punishment.

In contrast to the English KJV, neither the NIV nor the NASB translate hades as the word hell even once. They either translate hades/Hades as Hades, realm of the dead (footnoted as such in the NIV in several instances), or death. [NOTE: At the time of the publication of the first edition of this book, the NIV had translated Hades as depths (2) and grave (2) in lieu of realm of the dead or death/Hades in this same set of verses. That has since been changed by the publisher in another illustration of the dynamic nature of Bible translation as scholarship continues to advance.]

The above translations raise an interesting question: Were at least some of the mentions of Hades in the original Greek New Testament manuscripts allegorical references to the Greek god Hades for the purpose of illustration and hyperbole? It certainly appears that may have been the case, particularly in Revelation. Young's Literal Translation would also seem to indicate this might be the case. Take for example the following two verses:

> *And I tell you that you are Peter, and on this rock I will build my church, and the gates of Hades will not overcome it. (Matt 16:18)*

> *I looked, and there before me was a pale horse! Its rider was named Death, and Hades was following close behind him. They were given power over a fourth of the earth to kill by sword, famine and plague, and by the wild beasts of the earth. (Rev 6:8)*

Hades (the Greek god designated by the capital "H") guarded the gates of hades (the realm of the dead designated by a small "h") in the Greek religious system, of which both Jesus and the New Testament authors were intimately familiar. The Bible is filled with symbolic language and illustrations that many, if not most, Bible scholars agree are not to be taken literally. So the question becomes, which language and/or verses are we to take figuratively and which ones literally?

It is interesting that neither the NIV nor NASB EVER translate hades as hell. They leave it as Hades in all but a few verses where it is either translated as realm of the dead or death. In addition, there are no footnotes in either the NIV or NASB to indicate it means hell in any of the verses in which it occurs, even though the word hell occurs in a number of New Testament verses in both the NIV and NASB. What are we to make of this? If Hades means hell, why do/did the NIV and NASB translators feel compelled to leave it as Hades and not cross reference it to other mentions of hell in the New Testament?

It appears the secret to hell in our English Bibles lies with the early 5th century AD Latin Vulgate translation of hades. As you will recall, the LVB did not translate the Greek word gehenna to the pre-existing Roman notion of hell (inferus/infernum), but rather adopted gehenna into the Latin language as gehennae/gehennam. However, in the case of hades, the LVB translates it in all but one case as derivatives of the word inferus (including inferno and infernum), meaning "the lower place", "underneath" or "the underworld". Inferno is the Latin word from which our English word inferno, a raging fire, is derived. Inferno and infernum are defined as hell in many, if not most, Latin dictionaries. Is not a raging inferno the popular image of hell within orthodox Christianity?

It is clear the early Roman (Latin) Church agreed with the pagan Latin poets that hades was more than just the place where the dead go. It became a place of post mortem punishment.

Based upon this Roman pagan redefinition of the Greek word hades, around 400 AD some of the Roman Church fathers instrumental in translating the first Latin Bible (the Vulgate), ascribed hades, but apparently not gehenna, as a place of divine eternal punishment. As previously shown, the notion of eternity or everlastingness was concurrently being formulated around this time, and apparently in conjunction with this doctrine of eternal punishment for not adhering to the doctrines and dogma of a Church that was becoming an important institution of the state for controlling a collapsing Roman Empire.

The interesting thing about the LVB's translation of hades as the Latin conception of hell (inferus/infernum) is that Revelation 20:14 says both death and hades were cast into the "lake of fire". Many Christians believe hades IS the lake of fire! How can the lake of fire be cast into itself?

But, perhaps the most important observation is that the Roman Church interpretation of hades is in stark contrast to modern Bible translations, which **DO NOT** translate hades as hell. *In summary, there is a clear disagreement between the Latin Vulgate Bible and modern Bible translations as to which Greek word may be referring to the orthodox Christian notion of hell … gehenna or hades?*

Are you confused? Is it any wonder many people may have second thoughts about the traditional Christian notion of hell? If you are bewildered, you certainly have every right to be.

We'll only throw one more perplexing translation issue pertaining to the English word hell into the mix.

Tartarus – Origin and Usage

In the Greek system of pagan beliefs, tartarus was originally understood by the ancient Greek poets as a cosmic pit beneath the earth. It was the home of the Titan gods, Night and the storm winds. However, by roughly the 5th century BC, the

Greek philosophers and later poets came to view tartarus as the place where those who died and were judged (in hades) to have lived an evil life were sent for punishment. It roughly corresponded to the Christian concept of hell except that it was cold, not hot. Whether or not the Greeks believed punishment in tartarus to be of an eternal nature is unlikely, particularly in view of the concept of eternity being related to the later evolution of man's beliefs about God. However, as mentioned already, the much later Roman poets began to equate tartarus with hades. This association is significant, as we will see.

Hell and Tartarus in the New Testament

The good news (again, no pun intended) is the Greek word tartarus only occurs once in the entire New Testament.

> For if God did not spare angels when they sinned, but sent them to hell [tartarus], putting them into gloomy dungeons to be held for judgment; (2 Peter 2:4 NIV)

Looking back to the translation table for hell in the NIV baseline we can see it was either translated as hell (as in the NIV above) or left as tartarus (tartarum in the LVB). This would seem to be the most consistent translation of any of the hell words – gehenna, hades or tartarus.

The mitigating issue here is this verse is discussing God's fate for *angels*, not humans. The only Greek word that might ostensibly be associated with the modern Christian concept of punishment after death is not even being applied to humans! What are we to make of that? Additionally, for reasons already stated having to do with the evolution of the concept of eternity, it is highly unlikely that tartarus implied the notion of punishment being eternal in the Greek religious system or the Koine Greek language of the time.

To get to the heart of the issue pertaining to the duration of punishment in the afterlife, we have to understand the meaning and translation issues surrounding two other key Greek words – aion and aionios. Let's get started.

Aion and Aionios in the New Testament

Let's now turn our attention to two of the most contested words in the New Testament, the Greek words aion (sometimes also transliterated as aeon) and its adjectival form aionios. Aionios is the Greek adjective in the New Testament used to describe the punishment (represented by the Greek word "kolasin") that orthodox Christianity insists is eternal or everlasting for those who have not accepted Christ by the time of their death. The doctrine of eternal punishment is almost wholly predicated upon the translation of this single Greek word. But, is this what aionios really means?

In spite of orthodox Christianity's zealous historical defense of the doctrine of eternal punishment, most Christians are not aware there has been a contentious, long-standing issue surrounding the translation of both aion and aionios. This disagreement has spanned almost two millennia, the period from shortly after the writing of the original New Testament

Scriptures to the present. It is a complex issue I will try to simplify as much as possible. The facts are as follows.

The Greek word aion is the word from which our English word eon (a long, indefinite period of time) is derived.

It is generally agreed aion's translation as meaning an age or a long, indefinite period of time (an eon) was its *primary* meaning within the Koine Greek language.

Aion was the Koine Greek word used by the 70 Hebrew-Greek translators to *uniformly* translate (with one or two irrelevant exceptions) the Hebrew word olam in the Septuagint (often referred to as the LXX), the Koine Greek translation of the Hebrew Old Testament. As we have already discussed, olam in Hebrew meant hidden or unknown, but NOT eternal.

Aion has been translated to mean more than 20 different words/concepts in the New Testament in English Bibles. The definite, finite nature of many of the translated words/concepts is in direct opposition to the eternal, everlasting notion of others. Here is the list of words/concepts to which it is translated in the KJV and NASB New Testaments. Many modern translations are comparable to the NASB.

English Translation	KJV	NASB
age	2	20
ages		6
ancient time		1
beginning of time		1
course		1
eternal	2	2
eternity		1
ever	71	2
evermore	4	
forever		27
forever and ever		20

forevermore		2
long ago		1
miscellaneous	5	
never	6	1
old		1
time		1
world	38	7
worlds		1

Source: www.studylight.org New Testament Greek Lexicon

- Aionios, the adjectival form of aion, occurs 68 times in the NASB New Testament and has only been translated to mean eternal (66), eternity (1) or forever (1). Most modern translations are comparable.

- Young's Literal Translation, among others, translates aionios as "age-during" in all cases. This is the 19th century equivalent of "enduring/abiding for an age" or "of/for the age". It does NOT convey the notion of infinite time, eternity or endlessness.

What the New Testament authors meant when they used aion and aionios in the original manuscripts is of vital importance. The foundation of the orthodox doctrine of eternal punishment literally rests on the translation of aion and aionios, in addition to the three Greek "hell words" previously discussed.

Based upon the above facts, there are several questions and issues one might ask.

How did the Greek word aion have a singular meaning of finite but unknown time in the Greek Septuagint (circa 3rd century BC) but come to represent numerous words/concepts in the Greek New Testament (circa 70-100 AD) as translated in English Bibles 1500 years later?

In the KJV, how can aion mean both *never* AND *evermore* (i.e. always), Two completely opposite concepts?

In the New Testament, how can aion convey the notion of both a finite age and an endless eternity?

IF aion can convey both meanings, clearly context must have determined the translation that has been used. Given that, to what degree might the translator's theological predisposition have determined which notion was selected when either could have been used? That is the choice translators must make in all the New Testament verses where aion occurs and is translated to mean either a finite age or an endless eternity.

In light of these questions, I submit the following assertion for the reader's consideration.

It is difficult to conceive of any language, ancient or modern, using the same term to denote both a finite period of time and the opposing concept of eternity. Logic and reason suggest that any society sophisticated enough to comprehend the notion of eternity would also be sophisticated enough to create an unambiguous word to clearly communicate the concept. In English, we occasionally euphemistically use "forever" to describe something that will not literally last forever, as in "It took forever!" But ... do we ever use, even euphemistically, a term that denotes a finite period of time to also mean infinite time or eternity? I think not.

If aion could convey the notion of both a finite age and an endless eternity in the New Testament, why has aionios (an adjective derived from aion) ONLY been translated to supposedly convey the notion of eternal time or endlessness? Is this an indication of a pre-existing theological bias on the part of translators with respect to how aionios has been translated?

There is another argument made by some Bible scholars and experts in Greek that in the context of things related to God, aionios does not convey a notion of either finite time or eternity, but the notion that whatever it describes is of a divine nature. Thus, in the context of punishment, it would imply *divine* punishment, but not necessarily eternal punishment. Divine punishment would be that punishment administered by God in accordance with His divine sovereignty, mercy and justice.

Perhaps the most convincing argument for aionios **NOT** conveying the notion of something lasting forever (i.e. punishment) when it was written by the New Testament authors is the fact that there is historical documentation of aionios being used to convey a limited period of time both earlier, concurrent with, and after the original New Testament scriptures were written. Here are specific examples:

1. Before the New Testament

> *"The second wall is in all other respects like the first but of twice the height. The third circuit is rectangular in plan, and is sixty cubits in height, built of a stone hard and naturally durable (aionios)."* *[Diodorus Siculus, Library, book 17, chapter 71 section 5]*

2. Same general time period as the New Testament

> *"... as was Jonathon condemned to perpetual (aionios) imprisonment [Jonathon's incarceration was known to have lasted for 3 years]. And now the Romans set fire to the extreme parts of the city, and burnt them down, and entirely demolished its walls. [Flavius Josephus, The Wars of the Jews, Book 6, Section 434, as translated by William Whiston] [NOTE: Given the finite duration of Jonathon's incarceration, Whiston could have just as easily and perhaps more appropriately used the word "indefinite" or "indeterminate" in lieu of "perpetual".]*

3. Two hundred years after the New Testament

> *"Here again he means, that Satan occupies the space under Heaven, and that the incorporeal powers are spirits of the air, under his operation. For that his kingdom is eon enduring (aionios), in other words it will cease with the present eon, hear what he says at the end of the Epistle;"* [St. Chrysostum, Homily of the Epistle of Saint Paul to the Ephesians, Homily IV.]

The reader can find several works by various authors that further traces the etymology and history associated with the various New Testament words that are the subject of our discussion. Some of these works are well more than 100 years old and can be found at the following locations on the Internet.

http://www.tentmaker.org/books/Aion_lim.html

http://www.tentmaker.org/books/Aion.html

http://www.tentmaker.org/books/time/index.html

http://www.tentmaker.org/books/asw/index.html

Given the numerous questions about how the Greek words gehenna, hades, tartarus, aion and aionios have been translated in the New Testament, it will be helpful to now look at some of the key Bible passages most frequently cited in arguing the conditional Christian view of God's love, mercy, forgiveness and grace.

Key New Testament Parables

The Parable of the Sheep and Goats

Then they will go away to eternal punishment, but the righteous to eternal life. (Matt 25:46 NIV)

Many people consider Jesus' parable of the sheep and the goats (Matt 25:31-46 NIV) and its concluding verse, Matt 25:46, to be the "Rosetta Stone" of the argument for the Christian doctrine of eternal punishment for non-Christians. **It is the *ONLY* verse in the entire Bible where the phrase "eternal punishment" is alleged to have been used.**

If we delve further into the translation of this verse, we will see there are several questions that arise.

- Aionios is the Greek word translated as eternal in both instances in Matt 25:46 – i.e., eternal punishment and eternal life. As we have already discussed, many Bible scholars contend aionios did not mean eternal, but rather only the notion of enduring for an age (i.e. a long but unknown period of time) or being of a divine nature. In that light, the verse does not deny punishment, just that it does not last forever.

- If we think in terms of aionios implying a divine nature to the punishment as opposed to any temporal connotation, it again does not deny punishment, nor does it necessitate that it be eternal in duration. After all, God is sovereign in all things. Would this not also include the duration of any punishment He might deem warranted?

- Both of the preceding arguments equally apply to the reference to "eternal fire" in Matt 25:41, particularly in view of the fact that fire is a frequent metaphor used in the Bible for the notion of cleansing or purification.

- The Greek word translated to mean punishment in Matt 25:46 is *kolasin.* The original root word from which kolasin is derived means "to prune". In that context, kolasin conveys the notion of shaping or correction, not punishment. In fact, many Greek-English Bible dictionaries give "correction", not punishment, as the *primary* meaning of the word kolasin. The idea of correction carries no eternal connotation, only a temporal notion of remedial improvement. This provides a very different interpretation of Matt 25:46 that supports the view aionios may not have meant eternal.

- There is one final significant issue pertaining to Matt 25:46. In this parable, Jesus has traditionally been presumed to be discussing judgment and punishment of the righteous (sheep) and unrighteous (goats). If we take this parable literally, whether or not we will be rewarded with eternal life or eternally punished depends on whether we feed, quench the thirst, welcome as a stranger, clothe, and visit those sick or in prison ... "the least of these brothers of mine". He says nothing about believing in him or accepting him as our personal Lord and Savior, *the singular requirement by orthodox Christian doctrine* to avoid eternal punishment (i.e. salvation). To say the least, this is an interesting discontinuity between what Jesus is alleged to have asserted is required for salvation and that prescribed by traditional Christian doctrine.

Given this not insignificant number of issues surrounding the interpretation of Matt 25:46, how confident should we be that we can definitively assert it teaches eternal punishment beyond a reasonable doubt, *or at all?*

Lazarus and the Rich Man

This story, told by Jesus in the Gospel of Luke (Luke 16:19-31), is one of the key New Testament passages often cited by orthodox Christianity as literally and definitively teaching the doctrine of eternal punishment. But does it?

There are several points to consider in assessing this story and its message.

Many or most Bible scholars maintain this story is a parable, that Jesus did not intend for it to be interpreted literally, and that it has symbolic meaning far beyond the literal story. It is part of a series of five parables Jesus begins telling to "the Pharisees and teachers of the law" in Luke 15, and which are specifically described as parables in Luke 15:3.

The first four parables – the lost sheep, the lost coin, the prodigal son, the dishonest manager – are all directed at the lack of grace of the Jewish religious establishment toward sinners, and their dishonesty and greed in their dealings with the Jewish people.

The story contains a number of curious representations that would clearly seem more likely associated with a parable than a literal story – Abraham and the rich man can speak to each other between heaven and hell; the rich man can carry on a lucid conversation while being tortured by fire; the tip of Lazarus' finger dipped in water could cool the rich man's tongue; etc.

Many Bible translations do not refer to hell at all in this story. The NASB among others uses hades and does not footnote it as meaning hell. Other versions simply refer to it as the place or realm of the dead, but not hell.

So the question becomes what is the larger meaning of this story or parable?

There is at least one alternative interpretation that harmonizes with the other four parables Jesus told to the religious leaders at this same time. The rich man being dressed in purple (the color of royalty or prestige in the Jewish culture of the time) conveys the image that this was a member of the Jewish religious establishment. His failure to show compassion and provide help to the poor man alludes to how the religious elite had taken both financial and spiritual advantage of and ignored the legitimate needs of the Jewish people (i.e. Lazarus). The symbolic reward of Lazarus and punishment of the rich man is in harmony with Jesus' teachings in the beatitudes.

> *"Blessed are the poor in spirit, for theirs is the kingdom of heaven." (Matt 5:3)*

However, it is beyond the scope of this book to provide the definitive translation of this story. I only desire to apprise you that there are a number of good reasons to believe it is a parable, not a literal story about eternal punishment in hell, and that there are other more-than-reasonable interpretations.

Revelation: The Distorted Lens of Biblical Interpretation?

The Book of Revelation is, in many respects, an enigma within Christian theology. It has come to play a central role in contemporary Christianity yet, at the same time, it is overwhelmingly viewed as one of the most difficult to understand books in the Bible. This was one of several reasons that as much as 40 percent or more of the early Church fathers who are recorded as having commented on Revelation questioned its authenticity and authority.

According to tradition, John, the unknown author of both the Gospel and the epistles of John, is the author of Revelation. However, many Bible scholars believe another unknown author might have written this book. There are noticeable differences between the writing style, grammar and word usage between John's Gospel and other three epistles to those found in Revelation. It is the only book in the New Testament written in the style of Jewish apocalyptic literature and is filled with highly hyperbolic and symbolic language reminiscent of

Eastern culture and writing style, as opposed to the more constrained and rational narrative style of the Gospel and epistles of John.

Irrespective of its authorship, Revelation's meaning and interpretation has been contested throughout Christian history. Some significant Christians (e.g. Augustine, Martin Luther and John Calvin) viewed it, along with a few other books, as being of questionable or lesser canonical status to the Gospels, Acts and Pauline epistles. In spite of this history, today it is believed by many Christians to contain the most certain and graphic message as to the existence of hell and eternal punishment, as well as what will happen at the end of time when Christ returns. *In many respects, Revelation has become the lens through which many Christians interpret the entire Bible narrative.*

I do not believe it is an unreasonable question to ask whether a book that was questioned by so many highly regarded Christian leaders throughout history should occupy such a foundational role in contemporary Christian theology. Many Christians throughout history have offered arguably more rational and equally scriptural alternative interpretations of Revelation, or have viewed it as a book too difficult to definitively interpret or understand for it to serve as the authoritative basis of the cornerstone of the Christian view of how the world will end and the doctrine of hell and eternal punishment.

We have already discussed the fact that most Bible translations since the end of the 19th century omit any reference to hell in Revelation. The supposed inferences to hell and eternal punishment in Revelation primarily are derived from two mentions of the *"lake of fire"*, which is defined as the *"second death"* in Rev 20:14. In Rev 20:14-15, *"death and Hades"* and anyone whose name is not found in the *"book of life"* are thrown into the lake of fire. By direct substitution of the Rev

20:14 definition of the lake of fire, they experience the second death. The question becomes what is the second death? Unfortunately, it is not defined. However, other New Testament verses would appear to contradict the notion this second death is synonymous with eternal punishment.

> *The last enemy to be destroyed is death. (1 Cor 15:26 NIV)*

> *For I am convinced that neither death nor life, neither angels nor demons, neither the present nor the future, nor any powers, neither height nor depth, nor anything else in all creation, will be able to separate us from the love of God that is in Christ Jesus our Lord. (Rom 8:38-39 NIV)*

> *DEATH IS SWALLOWED UP in victory. (1 Cor 15:54 NIV)*

> *… we have put our hope in the living God, who is the Savior of all people, and especially of those who believe. (1 Tim 4:10 NIV)*

These are all Scriptures from the epistles of Paul. Was he wrong about death not being able to separate "us" from the love of God? Was he wrong about death being destroyed? Was he wrong about Jesus being "the Savior of all people, especially those who believe"? His explicit addition of "especially those who believe" to the end of 1 Tim 4:10 would clearly seem to mean he believed Jesus was the "Savior of *all people*", *believers* **AND** *everyone else*.

There is one other interesting item to discuss pertaining to the contested message of Revelation. There are seven references to "Abyss"/"abyss" or "bottomless pit" in English Bible translations of Revelation that may have contributed to the confusion around the issue of hell and eternal punishment. The references are translated from the Greek word *abussos*.

Abussos was the word used in the Septuagint to translate the Hebrew word *tehom*, which had the same meaning – an abyss, a deep or "bottomless" pit. Interestingly, the word occurs in the New Testament nine times – once in Luke 8:31, once in Romans 10:7, and seven times in Revelation (9:1, 2, 11; 11:7; 17:8; 20:1, 3).

Some orthodox Christian preachers and theologians have either explicitly taught or inferred that the word Abyss (abussos) in Revelation refers to hell. The problem with this is that Paul in Romans, when using the Greek word abussos, clearly specifies he is referring to the realm of the dead, and nothing more.

> *or 'WHO WILL DESCEND INTO THE ABYSS?'*
> *[that is, to bring Christ up from the dead]." (Rom 10:7 NIV)*

The above text enclosed in brackets is part of the actual translated verse in all Bibles, not my comments. Given that, there is no reason to believe Paul is referring to hell. In addition, the NIV Bible, as do many others, cross-references Romans 10:7 to Hebrews 13:20.

> *Now the God of peace, who brought up from the dead the great Shepherd of the sheep through the blood of the eternal covenant, even Jesus our Lord, (Heb 13:20 NIV)*

From this verse, we can clearly see the phrase "brought up from the dead" is referring to Christ's resurrection from the grave, not bringing him up from hell … unless **ALL** the dead go to hell, which is not in accord with Christian doctrine, orthodox or otherwise.

Consequently, it would seem difficult to contend abussos in Revelation meant anything other than where people, demons, the beast, etc. go when they die or are banished from this world. No reference to abussos (abyss) in any of the verses in which it appears in the New Testament denotes any notion of punishment, eternal or otherwise, only the cessation of existence in this world.

Now that we have discussed the enigmatic book of Revelation, let's discuss the last few issues pertaining to the New Testament.

Other New Testament Issues

For the sake of rounding out the alleged teaching of eternal punishment in the New Testament, the following table provides the number of occurrences and references to all reasonably related notions or concepts in the New International Version.

Notion or Concept	Occurs	Verses
Eternal/ forever/ everlasting punishment	1	Matt 25:46
Eternal/ forever/ everlasting damnation	0	
Eternal/ forever/ everlasting torment	0	
Eternal/ forever/ everlasting contempt	0	
Eternal/ forever fire	3	Matt 18:8, Matt 25:41, Jude 1:7
Lake of fire	2	Rev 20:14, Rev 20:15

It is interesting to note these six verses represent less than 1/1300th of the 7,957 verses in the New Testament. I don't think it is unreasonable to wonder why there are so few specific references in that portion of the Bible that ostensibly provides the most alleged support for one of the most significant doctrines in orthodox Christianity. Not only that, but there are a couple of issues even with these.

- Jude 1:6-7 is discussing the future judgment of angels, not people. It compares this judgment to the *destruction* of Sodom and Gomorrah who "serve as an example of those who suffer the punishment of eternal [aionios] fire". Sodom and Gomorrah were supposedly *destroyed* by burning sulfur (Gen 19:24), not *punished* by eternal fire. In addition, as already mentioned, they were or will be restored according to Ezekial (Ez 16:53).
- Rev 20:14 is talking about "death and Hades", not people, being cast into the lake of fire.

If these two verses are removed from our list above, the number of New Testament verses (not counting the 13-14 questionable hell verses) that one might argue refer to eternal punishment, not destruction, is *4 out of 7,957* New Testament verses — or just *1/2000th* of the total verses in the New Testament.

To be completely fair, there are a couple of other verses (Matt 25:30, Jude 1:13) that mention "darkness" in the context of it being the possible fate of some people after death. Only one of these describes it as ostensibly being "forever", again translated from the contested Greek word *aion*. Darkness is frequently used in the New Testament to describe people who do not know the truth or are not living in light. It would also seem there is a potentially substantive difference and contradiction in both darkness and eternal fire being used to describe the fate of sinners in the New Testament. Should the darkness verses be viewed as supporting the doctrine of eternal punishment? You be the judge.

Eternal Punishment vs. Destruction/Annihilation

And last but not least, it is worth noting that in the overall Bible there are almost as many verses that allegedly refer to God's divine punishment being destruction as opposed to eternal conscious torment (the scholarly theological term for eternal punishment). Christian denominations that adhere to this view (e.g. Jehovah's Witness, etc.) generally refer to this as *annihilation*. In the annihilationist view, an unbeliever simply ceases to exist in any form either in God's universe or His heavenly realm.

Destruction is the only punishment other than death mentioned in the Old Testament. In the New Testament, alleged eternal destruction would mean the forfeiture of eternal life. However, this would not seem to apply to the Old Testament since there was no developed notion of life after death in the Hebrew Scriptures.

Cascading Translation and Interpretation Errors

For the sake of full disclosure, I must point out that a number of Bible dictionaries and lexicons dispute the preceding assertions with respect to the definition of the key words we have been discussing and upon which the doctrine of eternal punishment rests. It is not my intention to malign the numerous valuable contributions of these works, but I must point out a flaw in the method by which many of these reference books have derived their meanings and/or interpretations.

Many if not most modern Bible reference books have primarily derived the meaning and interpretation of the original Hebrew and Greek words found in Scripture from the alleged meaning(s) and/or interpretation(s) of these words in the King James Bible, a number of which, as the preceding evidence suggests, have been mistranslated and/or misinterpreted in multiple instances. These reference books have not based the definitions and interpretations of these key Hebrew and Greek words on the socio-historical contextual meaning and usage at the time they were actually written by the original Bible authors. Instead, they have been directly or indirectly derived from the doctrinal understanding that was: 1) passed down from centuries dominated by the harsh Latin Vulgate translation, and 2) the limited availability and knowledge of the original Greek that existed at the time the KJV was published in 1611.

The traditional definitions and/or interpretations (as portrayed in the King James Bible) of the Hebrew and Greek words sheol, olam, gehenna, hades, tartarus, aion and aionios are classic examples of the problem of cascading errors resulting from meanings derived from a source in which the words had already been mistranslated and/or misinterpreted. That this should have occurred in the King James Bible is not hard to conceive when one considers that the KJV translators were heavily influenced by more than 1000 years of specific Church doctrines, many of which were sacrosanct (e.g. eternal punishment) at that time. After all, if God did not eternally punish sinners, how could the Church rationalize persecuting and killing heretics (which it continued to do for another 150-200 years after the KJV was published)? The subsequent adoption of the KJV as the standard Protestant Bible for the ensuing 400 years further served to reinforce these rigid doctrinal views. The result has been intransigent and perhaps biblically unsound doctrines that have arguably been excluded from serious and sincere examination in light of the socio-historical context and meanings of the original words and concepts.

Are you now even more confused? If you are, you have every right to be.

Let's now turn our attention to how a large number of the early Church fathers in the first few centuries understood God's ultimate plan with respect to His creation. This should give us further insight into what they understood the original, native language Scriptures to say.

A Brief History of the Early Church

Many people have little knowledge of early Christian history in the first several centuries after Christ. Irrespective of what you may or may not know about this period, there are a number of important facts that are typically overlooked or omitted by traditional accounts of early Church history. As you read this chapter, please bear in mind I am not trying to provide an exhaustive history of early Christianity. I am simply attempting to shed light on those facts regarding the early Church that have customarily been overlooked and have potentially significant implications pertaining to the subject of this book.

I will define the "early Church" to mean the Church as it evolved from the time of Jesus to the middle of the 6th century AD, a period of approximately 550 years or roughly 25 percent of Christian history. This 550-year span can be further divided into two distinct periods – 1) the early Church before it became the religion of the Roman Empire and 2) the Roman Church period that began with Emperor Constantine's Edict of Milan in 313 AD. This decree allowed the open practice of Christianity for the first time and paved the way for it to become the state religion of the Roman Empire within a few decades.

The Pre-Roman Church

Jesus lived and taught in Judah, the former southern kingdom of Israel, which had been conquered by a series of foreign empires beginning with, among others, Babylon in 587 BC, the Greeks (and various derived Hellenistic local cultures) in 331 BC, and lastly by Rome approximately 67 years before his birth. Though the Romans initially allowed the Jews to remain relatively separate and practice their religion among themselves, all of this changed in 70 AD when Jewish resistance to Roman subjugation prompted Rome to destroy and scatter the Jewish nation. From this point forward, Rome viewed Judaism and its embryonic offshoot, Christianity, as threats to its control and domination of its non-Roman subjects in the region. After that time, both Jews and Christians were persecuted and periodically arrested and tortured or killed by the Roman regime. As part of this persecution and suppression, Christian writings were routinely confiscated and burned in an attempt to eradicate the nascent faith. As a result of this repression and the normal passing of time, the number of early Christian writings available for study throughout most of Christian history was very limited. However, archaeological discoveries and a more methodical search for early Christian texts over the past 200 years have found more documents, providing additional insight into the history of the faith during these critical early centuries after Christ. It is in fact these discoveries that have led to some of the changes in modern Bible translations we have already discussed.

The key point we will examine about the pre-Roman Church is this: **Many, if not most, of the Greek-speaking early Church fathers believed God would ultimately restore ALL of His creation and All people to perfection through Christ. They believed this because of Scripture, not in spite of it.**

This belief is commonly referred to as *Universal Reconciliation*. The prevalence of Universal Reconciliation among the early Church fathers should be of interest to all Christians for any number of reasons, perhaps foremost among them the even more loving and inclusive nature portrayed by this earliest theological perspective of our Heavenly Father and the degree to which it arguably mirrors Jesus' beliefs about his own Abba, or Daddy.

Koine Greek was the common language uniting the earliest Christian communities east and south of the Mediterranean. This was precisely that part of the known world where Jesus and the Apostles preached and subsequently recorded the original Good News (in Koine Greek). It was also in this same geographic area that early Christianity spread most quickly as a result of the more pervasive northward persecution by Rome. For these reasons, it would seem obvious that **the Greek-speaking Church fathers of this era and from this area had the most intimate understanding and knowledge of the native language and nuances of the original New Testament Scriptures of any Christians in any later time or place**. Consequently, their beliefs should be of particular interest in our search for truth about the core message of Jesus and what ultimately became the New Testament Bible.

Universal Reconciliation is also referred to as Universal Restoration and Christian Universalism or, somewhat inaccurately, Universalism. Contrary to popular misperceptions of Universalism, the early Church fathers who believed in Universal Reconciliation (or Christian Universalism, as opposed to the more generic Universalism) did not deny God's judgment and punishment. They merely maintained that, according to their understanding of Scripture, *BECAUSE* He is a just and loving God His punishment would be remedial and temporary. Recognizing God's sovereignty in the administration of His infinite love, justice, mercy and grace, these Church fathers believed He would, in His infinite wisdom, determine just the right type and duration of punishment to individually reform each and every sinner. Most, if not all, even believed that ultimately Satan and the fallen angels would be reconciled to God. This may seem extreme until you reflect for a while on the omnipotent power of God and His love for *ALL* of His creation.

> *God saw all that he had made, and it was very good.*
> *(Gen 1:31 NIV)*

As we have seen and will continue to see, there are numerous scriptural and historical reasons to consider that Universal Reconciliation may have been the authentic teaching of Jesus in the Gospels, and the teaching of the Apostles and earliest disciples. The Gospels and epistles are replete with verses that appear to unambiguously assert it is God's purpose and will that ALL of His creation and All people be reconciled to Him, and there are no disputed words in these verses ... unless you dispute the meaning of *"all"* or how much of mankind *"the world"* includes. Ironically, contradicting all reason and logic, the Roman Church came to rationalize the word "all" in Scripture to mean something other than the totality of ALL and this has carried over into modern Christian doctrine though it is seldom mentioned. We will discuss this shortly.

It is not an overstatement to say Universal Reconciliation was almost certainly the dominant theology in the early Church. Four of the six Christian schools (Alexandria, Caesarea, Antioch, Edessa) founded in the first few centuries of the Church taught Universal Reconciliation for substantial portions, if not all, of their existence. Only Carthage, a Latin school, taught the notion of eternal punishment after death for sinners. Ephesus taught conditional immortality (i.e. annihilation of sinners).

The early Church fathers who ascribed to Universal Reconciliation were many of the most highly regarded Christian leaders of their time. They sincerely believed this was what the Hebrew Scriptures, Gospels and epistles taught, particularly the letters of Paul. They did not yet have the assembled orthodox Bible canon we read today, but they had copies of all the component texts.

The following is a list of some of the early Church leaders whose writings indicate they ascribed to the notion that God would ultimately redeem all of His creation and all people. The reader is directed to Appendix B for an extensive list of recorded passages from these historic figures.

St. Irenaeus, Bishop of Lyons (130-200 AD)
St. Pantaenus, 1st head of Didascaleion (c. 180 AD)
St. Clement of Alexandria (150-215 AD)
Origen (185-254 AD), "The Father of Theology"
Theophilus of Antioch (c. 168 AD)
St. Addai, 1st Bishop of Edessa (late 2nd century AD)
St. Gregory Thaumaturgus (213-270 AD)
St. Pamphilus of Caesarea (d. 309 AD)
Eusebius of Caesarea (260-341 AD)

St. Athanasius, "The Father of Orthodoxy" (296-373 AD)

Didymus the Blind (309-395 AD)

Diodore of Tarsus (320-394 AD)

St. Macrina the Younger (327-379 AD)

St. Basil the Great, Bishop of Caesarea (329-379 AD)

St. Gregory of Nazianzus, Bishop of Constantinople (330-390 AD)

St. Gregory of Nyssa, leading theologian of the Eastern Church (332-398 AD)

St. Ambrose, Bishop of Milan (340-397 AD)

St. Jerome (342-420 AD), created Latin Vulgate

St. John Chrysostom (347-407 AD)

Theodore of Mopsuestia (350-428 AD)

Theodoret the Blessed, Bishop of Cyrus (393-457 AD)

St. Hilary, Bishop of Poitiers (d. 363 AD)

Titus, Bishop of Bostra (b. 362-371 AD)

St. Cyril of Alexandria (c. 412 AD)

St. Peter Chrysologus, Bishop of Ravenna (406-450 AD)

St. Maximus of Turin(380-465 AD)

Olympiodorus, philosophical opponent of Justinian (c. 550 AD)

The key point to notice in the above list is these historic fathers in the early Church held some of the most prestigious positions and were widely admired and respected, even during the first century or more after the advent of the Roman Church in the 4th century AD. In addition, they are virtually uniformly favorably regarded to this day by what has become the modern Roman Catholic Church, as can be observed from the discussion of each at the official Catholic web site *NewAdvent.org*. It is important to note that it was the Roman Church of the time that declared a few of these legendary figures to be "anathema" many years, even centuries, after their death.

Origen is frequently but erroneously cited as the father of the doctrine of Universal Reconciliation. As can be seen from the above dates, the doctrine preceded him and can be historically traced back well into the 2nd century AD, if not before. In deed, a growing number of Bible scholars would contend the entire Bible narrative, and in particular the epistles of Paul, are most naturally and clearly understood to support the doctrine of Universal Reconciliation.

Origen lived during the period 185-254 AD. He is sometimes referred to as the Father of Theology and is generally recognized as having developed the first comprehensive and systematic Christian theology. Origen followed St. Pantaenus and St. Clement of Alexandria, both adherents to the doctrine of Universal Reconciliation, as the head of the Alexandrian Catechetical School (the Didascaleion), the leading pre-Roman school of Christian teaching. Tradition has it this school was the outgrowth of the Apostle and Gospel writer Mark's evangelism and teaching in Alexandria in the first century AD. Mark is also believed to have been instrumental in establishing the Christian school in Caesarea, which Origen also led at a later point.

Origen was revered as one of the greatest Christian teachers, a staunch defender of Christianity against paganism, and one of the most prolific writers of Christian theology and commentaries on the sacred books that came to comprise the Bible. It is not an exaggeration to say he was arguably the most dominant Christian figure of his time, and for a century or more thereafter. Many of the significant figures in the early Church during the 3rd and 4th centuries were students or adherents of Origen. Origen died a martyr in one of the Roman persecutions in the mid-3rd century after having authored an estimated several thousand Christian books and commentaries. Unfortunately, many of his works were lost when the Alexandrian library was destroyed by fire in the mid-fifth century. For an account of Origen's life and works, the reader is referred to the official Catholic Church website, http://www.newadvent.com. A flattering and apologetic article on Origen by the church whose forebears were complicit in his ultimately being declared "*anathema*" can be found at http://www.newadvent.org/cathen/11306b.htm.

The following are a few passages from some of the above early Church fathers with regard to God's plan to restore all people through Christ. More can be found in Appendix B.

> "*Wherefore also He drove him (Adam) out of Paradise, and removed him far from the tree of life, not because He envied him the tree of life, as some dare to assert, but because He pitied him and desired that he should not continue always a sinner, and that the sin which surrounded him should not be immortal, and the evil interminable and irremediable.*" – *St. Irenaeus, Bishop of Lyons*

> "*For that for which our Lord came into the world was altogether to teach and show that at the end of created things is a resurrection for all men. And at that time their acts of conduct will be represented on their own persons, and their bodies become volumes for the written things of justice, and there will not be he who knoweth not writing; because that every man shall read the letters of his own book at that day, and the account of his actions he taketh with the fingers of his hands.*" – *The Doctrine of Addai (c. late 2nd century – early 3rd century)*

"But we maintain, that the power of Christ's cross and of his death … is so great, that it will be sufficient for the healing and restoration of not only the present and future ages, but even for those of the past."–Origen

"… yet we hold that in the mind there is no evil so strong that it may not be overcome by the Supreme Word and God. For stronger than all the evils in the soul is the Word, and the healing power that swells in Him, and the healing He applies, according to the will of God to every man. The consummation of all things is the destruction of evil … " – Origen

"While the devil thought to kill One [Christ], he is deprived of all those cast out of hades, and he [the devil] sitting by the gates, sees all fettered beings led forth by the courage of the Saviour." – St. Athanasius

"Our Lord is the One who delivers man [all people], and who heals the inventor of evil himself [Satan]." and "For it is needful that evil should some day be wholly and absolutely removed out of the circle of being." – St. Gregory of Nyssa

"The wicked who have committed evil the whole period of their lives shall be punished till they learn that, by continuing in sin, they only continue in misery. And when, by this means, they shall have been brought to fear God, and to regard Him with good will, they shall obtain the enjoyment of His grace." – Theodore of Mopsuestia

"In the present life God is in all, for his nature is without limits, but is not all in all. But in the coming life, when mortality is at an end and immortality granted, and sin has no longer any place, God will

be all in all. For the Lord, who loves man, punishes medicinally, that he may check the course of impiety."—Theodoret the Blessed

The Roman Church

During the first five centuries of the early Church, neither Universal Reconciliation nor any of its proponents were condemned by any Church council or the vast majority of their Christian colleagues. However, after the Roman Empire adopted Christianity as the state religion, power and politics began to transcend faith and a sincere search for truth as the most important attributes of a successful clerical leader in the Church. As the power base of the Church began to shift toward the Latin-centric fathers in Rome and North Africa and away from the Greek-centric fathers of the eastern Mediterranean and Asia Minor, adherence to dogma increasingly became the litmus test for Church leaders, and this dogma was increasingly determined and at times dictated by the Roman power base within the Church. It was this shift of power that ultimately resulted in the Church splitting into multiple regional variants in the 5th century AD, and of which the Roman Catholic Church and the Eastern Orthodox Church became the two most dominant factions.

One point to consider with respect to the early Church's acceptance of Universal Reconciliation is that the two earliest Christian statements of faith, the Nicene Creed (381 AD) and the earlier Apostles' Creed (date unknown), did not contain any mention of the concept of eternal punishment.

The Nicene Creed (381 AD)	I believe in one God, the Father Almighty, Maker of heaven and earth, and of all things visible and invisible. And in one Lord Jesus Christ, the only-begotten Son of God, begotten of the Father before all worlds; God of God, Light of Light, very God of very God; begotten, not made, being of one substance with the Father, by whom all things were made. Who, for us men for our salvation, came down from heaven, and was incarnate by the Holy Spirit of the virgin Mary, and was made man; and was crucified also for us under Pontius Pilate; He suffered and was buried; and the third day He rose again, according to the Scriptures; and ascended into heaven, and sits on the right hand of the Father; and He shall come again, with glory, to judge the quick and the dead; whose kingdom shall have no end. And I believe in the Holy Ghost, the Lord and Giver of Life; who proceeds from the Father *and the Son*; who with the Father *and the Son* together is worshipped and glorified; who spoke by the prophets. And I believe one holy catholic and apostolic Church. I acknowledge one baptism for the remission of sins; and I look for the resurrection of the dead, and the life of the world to come. Amen
The Apostle's Creed (late 2nd century AD)	I believe in God, the Father Almighty, the Creator of heaven and earth, and in Jesus Christ, His only Son, our Lord: Who was conceived of the Holy Spirit, born of the Virgin Mary, suffered under Pontius Pilate, was crucified, died, and was buried. He descended into hell. The third day He arose again from the dead. He ascended into heaven and sits at the right hand of God the Father Almighty, whence He shall come to judge the living and the dead. I believe in the Holy Spirit, the holy catholic church, the communion of saints, the forgiveness of sins, the resurrection of the body, and life everlasting. Amen.

It is interesting to note that the earlier Apostle's Creed states that Jesus descended into "hell" before he rose on the third day. The original Latin word used was *inferos*, which as we have seen was the Latin word form used to translate the Greek word *hades* and which has most often been translated as hell in English Bibles. But, perhaps even more interesting, this statement was removed from the later Nicene Creed. In addition, the Nicene Creed specifically mentions that Jesus came *"for us men for our salvation"* and *"I look for the resurrection of the dead, and the life of the world to come"*, but makes no reference to eternal punishment for either sinners or unbelievers. If eternal punishment was a core doctrine of the Church at the time these creeds were formulated, one might think it would have been mentioned.

There is clear evidence Universal Reconciliation continued to be accepted, and not condemned, well into the 6th century. St. Augustine himself, the great orthodox Latin theologian of what became the Western or Roman Church, acknowledged the prevalence of this belief.

> *"There are **many** who though not denying the Holy Scriptures, do not believe in endless torments." – St. Augustine (354-430 AD), City of God*

Two other major Church figures echoed similar comments.

> *"I know that **most persons** understand by the story of Nineveh and its King, the ultimate forgiveness of the devil and all rational creatures."–St. Jerome (342-420 AD), primary translator and creator of the Latin Vulgate Bible*

> *"**The mass of men** say that there is to be an end of punishment to those who are punished."–St. Basil the Great, Bishop of Caesarea (329-379 AD)*

These passages clearly demonstrate Universal Reconciliation was a widely held view within the Church well into the 5th century. This may surprise those readers who have been led to believe that Christian Universalism is either a New Age belief or had been part of minority Gnostic beliefs discredited and rejected by the early Church in the first couple of centuries AD.

In addition to acknowledging the pervasiveness of Universal Reconciliation, Augustine also did not condemn it, calling it an *"amicable controversy"* and its adherents *"tender-hearted Christians"*. However, being from the harsher North African Latin school of thought and perhaps partly as a result of his pagan roots in the dualistic Manichean religion, Augustine believed in the endless punishment of the wicked. But, Augustine neither read nor wrote Greek. By reading only the Latin Vulgate Bible with key Greek words misinterpreted, perhaps his understanding of the original intent and meaning of the New Testament authors was skewed, or perhaps it was Augustine's acquiescence to the fact that the state religion, which Christianity had become by his time, simply could not tolerate a god more merciful than the state itself. Irrespective of what the case might be, I believe it is accurate to say it was Augustine's significant theological role in the increasingly politicized 5th century Church and the growing influence of the Latin Church within Christendom that propelled the belief in eternal punishment to ultimately become official doctrine in the 6th century.

In 544 AD, almost 300 years after the death of Origen, Roman Emperor Justinian directed Mennas, the Patriarch of Constantinople, to call a local council to condemn Origen and what Justinian declared to be errors in Origen's theology, including Universal Reconciliation. In his letter to Mennas, Justinian presents an argument against Universal Reconciliation, and concludes it with his declaration of the Church's official doctrine being eternal punishment of unbelievers. Writing in Greek, he wrote the following transliterated passage:

> *"The Holy Church of Christ teaches an endless aion-ion life to the righteous and endless punishment to the wicked."*

Arguably aware the Greek word aionios actually implied one or both of the concepts of "enduring for an age" or being of a divine nature, as opposed to the concept of eternity, Justinian qualified it with an *additional* Greek word that had later evolved to unambiguously convey the concept of endlessness. The Greek word he used to denote both eternal life and eternal punishment is *ateleutetos*. Interestingly, he omits the Greek word aionios entirely when describing eternal punishment, simply relying on the unambiguous ateleutetos. One might ask why aionios was not sufficiently clear to make his point regarding eternal punishment since it is the word that appears in Biblical scripture when discussing the supposed concepts of eternal life and punishment. However, to denote the endless life of the righteous, he prefixes aionios with the same ateleutetos. So, if aionios means endless or eternal as some theologians assert, when Justinian said "the Church teaches an endless aionion life to the righteous", did he mean to use the linguistically redundant phrase equivalent to "endless endlessness" or "eternal eternal" life? In addition, by omitting the word aionion in describing "endless punishment" but not "endless life", did he mean that endless life was of a divine nature but endless punishment was not? Is it not God that determines either according to orthodox doctrine? One other question: If aionios definitively meant endless or eternal at that time, why did he feel he needed to address this issue at all or use another Greek word to make his meaning clear?

It was not until the 5th Ecumenical Council called by Emperor Justinian in 553 AD in Constantinople that we see the first "official" condemnation of Universal Reconciliation and arguably its two major proponents—Origen (who led the Christian schools in both Alexandria and Caesarea and died more than 300 years earlier) and Theodore of Mopsuestia (who led the Christian school in Antioch and died more than 125 years earlier).

Though he was viewed by some as an able civil administrator, the official Catholic website www.NewAdvent.org describes Justinian as exercising "ecclesiastical tyranny". Evidencing this, he called this council for two purposes – to have the council acquiesce to his imperial decree of 544 AD that for the first time declared Origen, Theodore of Mopsuestia, and Universal Reconciliation as "anathema" (or heresy), and to resolve a few other doctrinal issues between the Eastern (Greek) and Western (Latin) churches. To call this an "ecumenical council", meaning a council of all the Church Bishops across Christendom, may well be a misnomer. Many Bishops refused to attend, including Pope Vigilius in Constantinople (the then headquarters of the Roman Church), because of 1) their objection to Emperor Justinian's attempts to establish Church doctrine by fiat, 2) disagreement with his decree, 3) disagreement with the post-mortem condemnation of those who had died in high esteem within the Church (i.e. Origen and Theodore), and 4) disagreements with each other. In spite of this and under what appears to have been pressure from Justinian, the council declared Origen and Theodore, as well as Theodoret the Blessed, anathema (i.e. excommunicated) and the belief in Universal Reconciliation as heresy against the Church.

This episode marked the beginning of the Christian Church's tragic legacy of persecuting other Christians and infidels for "heresy" against the Church. Over the next 1000 years, commonly called the Dark Ages, the Church all too frequently tortured or murdered anyone who denied its doctrines and dogma, and those who defied its politics. It ultimately became a crime punishable by death for anyone other than clergy to even possess a Bible.

One perspective on Justinian's ruthlessness toward those who disagreed with him or challenged the Roman state comes from Procopious, a prominent Eastern Roman scholar and historian during Justinian's reign who describes him as "cruel, venal, prodigal and incompetent". Procopius went on to write:

> "No one but God, I believe, could count those he murdered."

Sadly, this decline of the Roman Church into an intolerant, cruel, political, manipulative, greedy and corrupt enterprise marked the arc of Christianity in the West for the next **1000 years**. Beginning in the 16th century AD, the Reformation finally began the process of addressing *some* of these unsavory aspects of the Church, but initially at least fell far short of addressing all of them.

Hopefully this brief insight into the early Church has provided a reasoned basis as to why Christians searching for truth should further investigate the traditional view of God's nature, purpose and will, and the history and traditions from which it emerged.

Let's now turn our attention to those portions of New Testament Scripture that led so many of the early Church fathers to believe God would ultimately restore all of His creation and reconcile all people to Himself.

Universal Reconciliation in the New Testament

Jesus' teachings about God are the primary focus of the New Testament. Consequently, it is important we frame Jesus' teachings in light of the circumstances in which he lived and taught.

Jesus was born and died a Jew. During his childhood, he was well trained in Jewish Law and the Scriptures. As a man and itinerant rabbi, he defied both the religious leaders of his time and Jewish Law, which had come to define righteousness and one's hope for salvation within Jewish society. Jesus' strongest invectives were reserved for the Jewish religious establishment, principally the Pharisees and Sadducees, who he believed were hypocrites misleading the Jewish people by misrepresenting God and filling their own coffers with wealth derived from the sacrifices of the poor. In opposition to the false pride and harsh piety of the Jewish leaders, Jesus brought a radical message of God's love, mercy, forgiveness and grace that defied the traditional portrayal of an angry, vengeful God that demands sacrifices and dispenses severe punishment for any sin.

Jesus' Theology

Jesus described God as Father more than 170 times in the Gospels. He gave this characterization of God far more weight than any other. In numerous instances, Jesus referred to God as "Abba", or Daddy, the most intimate Aramaic term of adoration for his and our Father. This image of God was arguably the very core of Jesus' theology. If Jesus is right and God is the Heavenly Abba of all people, it is hard to fathom how He could punish any of His children forever. Certainly no one can conceive of an earthly father who would do this. But for some reason, it doesn't seem to present traditional Christianity a problem that our Heavenly Father can or would. If man is made in God's image as Genesis 9:6 tells us, how are we to believe God would be less merciful and compassionate than a perfect earthly father? Must God not be MORE perfect than the very best human father?

To simply assert God is holy and just and, as a result, eternal punishment is what the Bible teaches is not a satisfying answer to many people, including many committed and conscientious Christians. Logically, this trite and simplistic explanation should be even more uncomfortable now that we have seen the serious questions surrounding those miniscule portions of Scripture that supposedly declare that a loving, merciful and just God *intentionally* subjects the vast majority of humanity to eternal conscious torment.

In a clear attempt to describe a more gracious understanding of a loving, forgiving God, Jesus tells us:

> *'But I tell you: Love your enemies and pray for those who persecute you, that you may be sons of your Father in heaven. He causes his sun to rise on the evil and the good, and sends rain on the righteous and the*

unrighteous. ... Be perfect, therefore, as your heavenly Father is perfect.' (Matt 5:43-48 NIV)

Then Peter came and said to Him, "Lord, how often shall my brother sin against me and I forgive him? Up to seven times?" Jesus said to him, "I do not say to you, up to seven times, but up to seventy times seven." (Matt 18:22 NASB)

Clearly in this last verse, Jesus is not literally saying we should forgive someone 490 times ("seventy times seven") and then cease to forgive them after that. Isn't he saying God calls us to *always* forgive our enemies ... and those who persecute us? If God calls us to do this, could He in His perfect love, justice, mercy, forgiveness and grace not do it Himself?

In our discussion of Jesus' life and teachings, there is another interesting set of verses we should consider that are often overlooked as to their seemingly clear meaning that appears to be in opposition to traditional doctrine. In Matthew 22 Jesus is being questioned by the Pharisees and a religious expert as to the most important commandment under the Law, he replies,

'Love the Lord your God with all your heart and with all your soul and with all your mind.' This is the first and greatest commandment. And the second is like it: 'Love your neighbor as yourself.' All the Law and the Prophets hang on these two commandments.' (Matt 22:37-40 NIV)

If we take Jesus at his word, everything else is secondary to these two commandments ... *everything*, including presumably our orthodox Christian doctrine of salvation that requires we accept Jesus as our personal Lord and Savior *in this life*. Jesus himself seems to contradict this in so many words elsewhere in Scripture.

And everyone who speaks a word against the Son of Man will be forgiven, but anyone who blasphemes against the Holy Spirit will not be forgiven. (Luke 12:10 NIV)

I tell you the truth, all the sins and blasphemies of men will be forgiven them. But whoever blasphemes against the Holy Spirit will never be forgiven; he is guilty of an eternal sin. (Mark 3:28-29 NIV)

(For what it's worth, aionios is the Greek word translated as eternal in Mark 3:29. You should be well familiar with the issues surrounding aionios at this point.)

According to Jesus in Luke, blaspheming the Son of Man (Jesus) will be forgiven, but blaspheming the Holy Spirit is a different story. I think most Christians believe denying Jesus as Lord and Savior constitutes blasphemy against him, yet Jesus says it will be forgiven. If that is the case, this verse, like Matt 25:46, would appear to be in opposition to orthodox Christian doctrine, which maintains the only unforgivable sin is not accepting Jesus Christ before we die, not blaspheming the Holy Spirit.

Both verses say blaspheming the Holy Spirit will not be forgiven. Presumably this means by God. However, notice it specifically does not say this blasphemy will be punished forever; it just says it will not be forgiven. What should we make of that? Is it simply a mark blasphemers will forever bear in God's sight? Should we read these words with a predisposition toward eternal punishment? We have already pointed out the very real issues surrounding the key words upon which that doctrine rests. Or, should we simply read the words Jesus allegedly spoke and not go beyond them? Who is to say?

Before we continue, it is also worth noting this lack of forgiveness by God for blasphemy against the Holy Spirit appears to conflict with a number of other verses in the Bible – Isa 43:25, Jer 31:34, 2 Cor 5:18-19, Heb 7:27, Heb 8:12, Heb 10:12, Heb 10:17, 1 Pet 3:18, 1 John 1:7, 1 John 1:9, 1 John 2:2 – to name a few. All of these verses, among others, say that God will ultimately forgive men's sins ... all of them. What are we to make of that?

As we will now see, there is much in the Gospels and the entire New Testament that appears to contradict the traditional Christian doctrine of eternal conscious torment and describes a more merciful, forgiving and just God. This is precisely how many or most early Church fathers literate in the native Greek of the New Testament apparently read the Scriptures and understood Jesus' message about God's nature, purpose and will. So, from what Scriptures did they derive this belief in and scriptural authority for Universal Reconciliation?

God's Purpose and Will: To Restore All

As we have shown, the early Church fathers who believed in Universal Reconciliation believed it was God's purpose and will to restore all of His creation and all people to Himself in the fullness of time. They believed this because of what they understood Scripture to say, not in spite of it. Here are a few verses of New Testament Scripture from which they might have found authority for this belief. I list them generally in the order in which they occur in the New Testament, not by any particular significance.

> '... If a man owns a hundred sheep, and one of them wanders away, will he not leave the ninety-nine on the hills and go to look for the one that wandered off? And if he finds it, I tell you the truth, he is happier about that one sheep than about the ninety-nine that did not wander off. In the same way your Father

in heaven is not willing that any of these little ones should be lost.' (Matt 18:12-14 NIV)

But the angel said to them, 'Do not be afraid. I bring you good news of great joy that will be for all the people.' (Luke 2:10 NIV)

For my eyes have seen your salvation, which you have prepared in the sight of all people, a light for revelation to the Gentiles and for glory to your people Israel. (Luke 2:30-32 NIV)

... and that he [God] may send the Christ, who has been appointed for you — even Jesus. He must remain in heaven until the time comes for God to restore everything, as he promised long ago through his holy prophets. (Acts 3:20-21 NIV)

And you are heirs of the prophets and of the covenant God made with your fathers. He said to Abraham, 'Through your offspring all peoples on earth will be blessed.' (Acts 3:25 NIV)

The above verse is a reference to Old Testament Scripture in which God tells Abraham and his descendants it is through them that all nations and peoples will be blessed. He does this no less than five times in Genesis alone, and it is mentioned in several other places throughout the Bible as well. The Jews clearly understood themselves to have been God's "chosen people", but the question is ... "Chosen for what?" These verses would seem to indicate God selected the Jews for the specific *purpose* of bringing His blessing to all nations and people, NOT merely for *privilege*.

Here are a few more verses alluding to God's plan.

For this is what the Lord has commanded us: 'I have made you a light for the Gentiles [all other people],

*that you may bring salvation to the ends of the earth.'
(Acts 13:47 NIV)*

*... I worship the God of our fathers as a follower
of the Way, ... and I have the same hope in God as
these men, that there will be a resurrection of both
the righteous and the wicked. [Said by Paul at his
trial before Felix, governor of Caesarea] (Acts 24:14-
15 NIV)*

*And he [God] made known to us the mystery of his
will according to his good pleasure, which he purposed in Christ, to be put into effect when the times
will have reached their fulfillment —to bring all
things in heaven and on earth together under one
head, even Christ. (Eph 1:9-10 NIV)*

*For this is good and acceptable in the sight of God our
Saviour; Who will have all people to be saved, and
to come unto the knowledge of the truth. For there is
one God, and one mediator between God and men,
the man Christ Jesus; Who gave himself a ransom for
all, to be testified in due time.... (1 Tim 2:3-6 KJV)*

*This is a trustworthy saying that deserves full accep-
tance. That is why we labor and strive, because we
have put our hope in the living God, who is the Savior of all people, and especially of those who believe.
(1 Tim 4:9-10 NIV)*

*For the grace of God has appeared that offers salva-
tion to all people. (Titus 2:11 NIV)*

Could it be that God's purpose and will of salvation for all is an even more magnificent message of "Good News" than the traditional Christian Gospel has proclaimed?

God Sent Jesus To Save the World (All People)

The early Church fathers who believed in Universal Reconciliation thought God sent Jesus to save *the **entire** world* from its sins, including *all people*, not just an elect few. They may well have found authority for this belief in the following verses.

> 'The Son of Man came to seek and save what was lost.' *(Luke 19:10 NIV)*

> The next day John [the Baptist] saw Jesus coming toward him and said, 'Look, the Lamb of God, who takes away the sin of the world!' *(John 1:29 NIV)*

> For God so loved the world that he gave his one and only Son, that whoever believes in him shall not perish but have eternal life. *(John 3:16 NIV)*

John 3:16 is one of the key verses Christianity has traditionally interpreted to support the doctrine that only through authentic belief in Jesus Christ *in this life* will a person avoid eternal punishment. However, if we examine the verse closely, we discover some interesting things. It says nothing about punishment, though it does mention perishing. However, it would seem difficult for one to be eternally punished if he or she perishes. It does speak to achieving eternal (aionios is again the Greek word used) life through belief in Jesus Christ. In light of the issues surrounding aionios, might aionion life perhaps be better understood as the divine nature of life achieved through Christ as opposed to simply the notion of endless life?

The verse that immediately follows John 3:16 is striking in that it seems to convey a clear sentiment consistent with Universal Reconciliation.

> *For God did not send his Son into the world to condemn the world, but to save the world through him. (John 3:17 NIV)*

Is it reasonable to argue that "world" in this verse does not encompass all people? How should the immediate proximity of this verse affect the traditional Christian interpretation of John 3:16?

Here are a few more verses pertaining to Jesus' role in God's plan to restore His creation.

> *'I am the good shepherd; I know my sheep and my sheep know me — just as the Father knows me and I know the Father — and I lay down my life for the sheep. I have other sheep that are not of this sheep pen. I must bring them also. They too will listen to my voice, and there shall be one flock and one shepherd.' (John 10:14-16 NIV)*

> *'Father, the time has come. Glorify your Son, that your Son may glorify you. For you granted him authority over all people that he might give eternal life to all those you have given him.' (John 17:1-2 NIV)*

> *… just as one trespass [Adam's sin against God] resulted in condemnation for all people, so also one righteous act [Jesus' taking on the sins of the world] resulted in justification and life for all people. (Rom 5:18 NIV)*

> *For as in Adam all die, so in Christ all will be made alive. (1 Cor 15:20 NIV)*

But our citizenship is in heaven. And we eagerly await a Savior from there, the Lord Jesus Christ, who, by the power that enables him to bring everything under his control, will transform our lowly bodies so that they will be like his glorious body. (Phil 3:20-21NIV)

For God was pleased to have all his fullness dwell in him [Jesus], and through him to reconcile to himself all things, whether things on earth or things in heaven, ... (Col 1:19-20 NIV)

He is the atoning sacrifice for our sins, and not only for ours but also for the sins of the whole world. (1 John 2:2 NIV)

And we have seen and testify that the Father has sent his Son to be the Savior of the world. (1 John 4:14 NIV)

But we see Jesus, who was made a little lower than the angels, now crowned with glory and honor because he suffered death, so that by the grace of God he might taste death for everyone. (Heb 2:9 NIV)

All People Will Be Reconciled to Go

The early Church fathers who believed in Universal Reconciliation believed all sin would ultimately be forgiven, its stain upon mankind would be removed forever, death would be eliminated from God's creation, and all people would be reconciled to God. However, contrary to the customary Christian arguments against Universal Reconciliation, *the ultimate reconciliation of all things DOES NOT preclude judgment and punishment as part of the process*. Scripture assures this reconciliation, and most often through Christ as a mediator.

All mankind will see God's salvation. (Luke 3:6 NIV)

'But I [Jesus], when I am lifted up from the earth, I will draw all people to myself.' (John 12:32 NIV)

All this is from God, who reconciled us to himself through Christ and gave us the ministry of reconciliation: that God was reconciling the world to himself in Christ, not counting men's sins against them. And he has committed to us the message of reconciliation. (2 Cor 5:18-19 NIV)

He is not the God of the dead, but of the living, for to him all are alive." (Luke 20:38 NIV)

Jesus said, 'Father, forgive them, for they do not know what they are doing.'" (Luke 23:34 NIV)

This last verse is worth a special comment. Are we to doubt that God forgave those that Jesus specifically asked Him to forgive with literally his dying breath ... those who demonstrated the ultimate rejection of Christ by crucifying him on the cross in the most brutal, blasphemous way imaginable? If God forgave this rejection of both Him and Jesus Christ, whom else might He forgive?

The Lord is not slack concerning his promise, as some men count slackness; but is longsuffering to us-ward, not willing that any should perish, but that all should come to repentance. (2 Peter 3:9 KJV)

This last verse beautifully describes God's "longsuffering" toward men in order to redeem them. One has to wonder if an infinite God's longsuffering would be limited to the relatively short life of a man. It is also another case where perishing is seemingly contrasted with the aionion life available through sincere repentance and acceptance of Jesus Christ. In using the word perishing, might the New Testament authors have been referring to man's inability at any particular time to avail him or herself of the divine (aionios) life available through Christ?

Death Is Not the End to God's Grace

Since clearly not all people come to know God and/or accept Jesus Christ prior to death, God's ability to redeem and reconcile all people to Himself is only possible if His love, justice, mercy, forgiveness and grace extend beyond death and the grave. Clearly that would not be a problem for a sovereign, omnipotent and transcendent God. It is simply a matter of His will. We've already seen numerous verses that appear to address God's will to save all people. Presumably *all* would have to mean irrespective of their belief at the time of their death. So, by what Biblical authority did the early Church fathers believe God might actually do this? Here are a couple of New Testament verses indicating God may in fact do precisely that.

> For I am convinced that neither death nor life, neither angels nor demons, neither the present nor the future, nor any powers, neither height nor depth, nor anything else in all creation, will be able to separate us from the love of God that is in Christ Jesus our Lord. (Rom 8:38-39 NIV)

Is it just coincidental that Paul mentions death as the very first item in his list of things that cannot separate us from the love of God? Or, that he finally concludes his list with the all encompassing "nor anything else in all creation"? That would not seem to leave anything, including man's rebellion against God or Jesus, to prevent His love from ultimately reaching and transforming every person.

Let's look at another Pauline verse.

> *Therefore God exalted him to the highest place and gave him the name that is above every name, that at the name of Jesus every knee should bow, in heaven and on earth and under the earth, and every tongue confess that Jesus Christ is Lord, to the glory of God the Father. (Phil 2:9-11 NIV)*

In the above passage, Paul would seem to have in mind that at some point every person, without exception, would ultimately come to acknowledge and accept Jesus Christ as Lord and Savior. It also seems that by "under the earth" he may be using the first century colloquialism referring to those who have died. Presumably "every knee" and "every tongue" would include all people, irrespective of their acceptance of Jesus Christ at the time of their death.

In the following verse Paul seems to clearly be saying that if our hope in Jesus Christ is limited to this life only, then we are to be sorely pitied. It would seem to indicate Paul firmly believed Christ's ability to reconcile us to him is not constrained by the boundary of death to this worldly existence.

> *If only for this life we have hope in Christ, we are of all people most to be pitied (1 Cor 15:19 NIV).*

The following is a verse from Revelation that would seem to be making essentially the same point.

> *Then I heard every creature in heaven and on earth and under the earth and on the sea, and all that is in them, singing: 'To him who sits on the throne and to the Lamb be praise and honor and glory and power, for ever and ever!' (Rev 5:13 NIV)*

It would seem to logically follow that if all people, living or dead, ultimately come to accept Jesus Christ as their Lord and Savior (Phil 2:9-11 and Rev 5:13) and nothing, including death, can separate us from God's love (Rom 8:38-39), then everyone would ultimately be redeemed and transformed by Christ and reconciled with God such that His creation is once again holy and perfect – or *"all in all"*.

As you can see, there are a number of New Testament verses that seem to paint a picture of a God that continues to work beyond man's sliver of earthly existence to reunite all of His creation to Him.

God Will Once Again Be "All in All"

The following passage from Paul in 1 Corinthians is frequently referenced by many of the early Church fathers who believed in Universal Reconciliation, as well as many Christians throughout history and today, to arguably be the clearest Bible passage describing the process by which all people and the world will ultimately be reconciled to God at the end of time. There are numerous references in early Christian writings throughout history to God being "all in all".

> *For as in Adam all die, so in Christ all will be made alive. But each in his own turn: Christ, the first fruits; then, when he comes, those who belong to him. Then the end will come, when he hands over the kingdom to God the Father after he has destroyed all dominion, authority and power. For he must reign until he has put all his enemies under his feet. The last enemy to be destroyed is death. For he 'has put everything under his feet.'. Now when it says that "everything" has been put under him, it is clear that this does not include God himself, who put*

everything under Christ. When he has done this, then
the Son himself will be made subject to him who put
everything under him, so that God may be all in all.
(1 Cor 15:22-28 NIV)

If God is to once again be "all in all" as Paul claims, it would seem difficult for that to happen if the vast majority of mankind is subjected to eternal punishment or annihilation. Not only that, as we saw above in John 17:1-2, Jesus said his Father gave him *"authority over all people"*, which would presumably mean all people are included in "those who belong to him". It is also interesting to note in the above verses that *"after he has destroyed all dominion, authority and power"* would seem to be speaking to the earthly kingdoms and power structures that Jesus spoke most passionately against, not individual people … and these institutions are being destroyed, eliminated from God's creation, not punished forever. And finally, even death itself is destroyed which would seem to imply if there remained any who were dead they would be brought back to life, yet another opportunity by which God's inescapable love might ultimately redeem them. What else could God becoming "all in all" mean?

New Testament Parables

There are several parables Jesus tells in the New Testament that the early Church fathers who believed in Universal Reconciliation may have understood to teach the ultimate restoration of all things through Christ. I will discuss a few of these in no particular order.

The Parable of the Prodigal Son

One of the most beautiful parables in the Bible is the parable Jesus tells of the prodigal son found in Luke 15:11-32. For your convenience, here's the story from the NIV Bible:

Jesus continued: "There was a man who had two sons. The younger one said to his father, 'Father, give me my share of the estate.' So he divided his property between them. "Not long after that, the younger son got together all he had, set off for a distant country and there squandered his wealth in wild living. After he had spent everything, there was a severe famine in that whole country, and he began to be in need. So he went and hired himself out to a citizen of that country, who sent him to his fields to feed pigs. He longed to fill his stomach with the pods that the pigs were eating, but no one gave him anything. "When he came to his senses, he said, 'How many of my father's hired men have food to spare, and here I am starving to death! I will set out and go back to my father and say to him: Father, I have sinned against heaven and against you. I am no longer worthy to be called your son; make me like one of your hired men.' So he got up and went to his father. "But while he was still a long way off, his father saw him and was filled with compassion for him; he ran to his son, threw his arms around him and kissed him. "The son said to him, 'Father, I have sinned against heaven and against you. I am no longer worthy to be called your son.' "But the father said to his servants, 'Quick! Bring the best robe and put it on him. Put a ring on his finger and sandals on his feet. Bring the fattened calf and kill it. Let's have a feast and celebrate. For this son of mine was dead and is alive again; he was lost and is found.' So they began to celebrate.

"Meanwhile, the older son was in the field. When he came near the house, he heard music and dancing. So he called one of the servants and asked him what was going on. 'Your brother has come,' he replied, 'and your father has killed the fattened calf because he has him back safe and sound.' "The older brother became angry and refused to go in. So his father went out and pleaded with him. But he answered his father, 'Look! All these years I've been slaving for you and never disobeyed your orders. Yet you never gave me even a young goat so I could celebrate with my friends. But when this son of yours who has squandered your property with prostitutes comes home, you kill the fattened calf for him!' " 'My son,' the father said, 'you are always with me, and everything I have is yours. But we had to celebrate and be glad, because this brother of yours was dead and is alive again; he was lost and is found.' "

Most Christians understand this story to symbolize people's rebellion against God and His unconditional love, patience, forgiveness and reconciliation upon their sincere repentance and confession of their sins and return to Him. There are a couple of interesting questions or points to be made regarding this parable:

How long would the father have waited for his lost son to return?

What does the resentfully obedient older brother's anger and jealousy represent with respect to the father's acceptance and forgiveness of the son who returned?

Regarding the parable narrative, I think most people would agree the father would have waited with open arms until the day he died for his prodigal son to return. Since God is not mortal, what does that say about His unconditional love, acceptance and patience for His children? How long will a longsuffering God wait?

Most explanations of the parable associate the jealous older brother with the Pharisees and Sadducees of Jesus time. They lived outwardly righteous lives but refused to show grace to sinners. It is interesting to consider whether the Pharisees' and Sadducees' misunderstanding of God's grace might equally apply to Christians throughout history and even today, who believe, either explicitly or implicitly, that God's grace is a reward for their *act* of faith. **Is making God's grace conditional upon specific faith in this life inconsistent, or an oxymoron?** Apparently many of the early Church fathers believed the Greek New Testament Scriptures taught that it was.

The Parable of the Lost Sheep

Like the parable of the prodigal son, the parable of the lost sheep told by Jesus in Luke 15:1-7 is another story which reasserts God's joy in saving those who are lost. The following is from the NIV Bible:

> Now the tax collectors and "sinners" were all gathering around to hear him. But the Pharisees and the teachers of the law muttered, "This man welcomes sinners and eats with them." Then Jesus told them this parable: "Suppose one of you has a hundred sheep and loses one of them. Does he not leave the ninety-nine in the open country and go after the lost sheep until he finds it? And when he finds it, he joyfully puts it on his shoulders and goes home. Then he calls his friends and neighbors together and says, 'Rejoice with me; I have found my lost sheep.' I tell you that in the same way there will be more rejoicing in heaven

over one sinner who repents than over ninety-nine
righteous persons who do not need to repent.

The meaning of this parable would seem to be apparent … God rejoices in saving sinners. Like the prodigal son story, a similar question is raised as to how long the shepherd would search for his lost sheep. The parable clearly answers this question with … *"until he finds it."* Since the message of *the Bible is relevant to all times and places*, this raises an interesting point to consider: **How are we to understand "until he finds it" in terms of God's unconditional love for His children?**

The early Church fathers who taught Universal Reconciliation must have believed this parable described a God that would never quit searching for His lost sheep. As many of their recorded writings convey, as well as those of Paul in Rom 8:38-39, they believed Jesus' power to redeem sinners extends beyond death and the grave.

The parable of the lost coin in Luke 15:8-10 is a very similar parable to the lost sheep. Consequently, we will not further belabor these same points and questions.

The Parable of the Landowner and Vineyard Workers

The parable of the landowner and vineyard workers in Matthew 20:1-16 is a follow-on to Jesus' discussion at the end of Matthew 19 with the young rich man as to who will be first and who will be last into God's kingdom. He mentions eternal (i.e. aionion) life but says nothing of punishment or destruction, eternal or otherwise. Interestingly, in Matt 19:28, Jesus uses the phrase "at the renewal of *all things*", seemingly consistent with the theme of Universal Reconciliation. Here's the NIV version of the landowner and vineyard workers.

"For the kingdom of heaven is like a landowner who went out early in the morning to hire men to work in his vineyard. He agreed to pay them a denarius for the day and sent them into his vineyard. "About the third hour he went out and saw others standing in the marketplace doing nothing. He told them, 'You also go and work in my vineyard, and I will pay you whatever is right.' So they went. He went out again about the sixth hour and the ninth hour and did the same thing. About the eleventh hour he went out and found still others standing around. He asked them, 'Why have you been standing here all day long doing nothing?' " 'Because no one has hired us,' they answered." He said to them, 'You also go and work in my vineyard.' "When evening came, the owner of the vineyard said to his foreman, 'Call the workers and pay them their wages, beginning with the last ones hired and going on to the first.' "The workers who were hired about the eleventh hour came and each received a denarius. So when those came who were hired first, they expected to receive more. But each one of them also received a denarius. When they received it, they began to grumble against the land-owner. 'These men who were hired last worked only one hour,' they said, 'and you have made them equal to us who have borne the burden of the work and the heat of the day.' "But he answered one of them, 'Friend, I am not being unfair to you. Didn't you agree to work for a denarius? Take your pay and go. I want to give the man who was hired last the same as I gave you. Don't I have the right to do what I want with my own money? Or are you envious because I am generous?' "So the last will be first, and the first will be last."

Most Christians agree this parable is a story making the point that grace is not earned, but is given by God in His sovereign mercy. If that is true, it would seem to follow that, as with the vineyard workers' compensation, God could choose to provide His grace to all people at any time of His choosing, before or after death. Could that be the inspiration the early Church fathers who believed in Universal Reconciliation received from this parable?

Ties to the Old Testament

Before we wrap up this chapter on some of the New Testament verses that would seem to support the belief that God's plan may be, and always has been, to ultimately restore all of His creation and people to Himself, let me just once again demonstrate this notion was present in the Old Testament, even if not as fully developed as in the New Testament.

> ..., *so we must die. But God does not take away life; instead, he devises ways so that a banished person may not remain estranged from him. (2 Sam 14:14 NIV)*
>
> *and the dust returns to the ground it came from, and the spirit returns to God who gave it. (Ecc 12:7 NIV)*
>
> *... he [God] will destroy the shroud that enfolds all peoples, the sheet that covers all nations; he will swallow up death forever. (Isa 25:7-8 NIV)*
>
> *he [God] says: 'It is too small a thing for you to be my servant to restore the tribes of Jacob and bring back those of Israel I have kept. I will also make you a light for the Gentiles [everyone else], that you may bring my salvation to the ends of the earth.' (Isa 49:6 NIV NIV)*

I don't know about you, but I have often struggled with harmonizing the Old Testament with the New. It is my strong conviction that Universal Reconciliation seems to go a long way in reconciling these two very different portions of the Bible.

New Testament Summary

As you can see, there are many, many New Testament verses and parables that appear to teach the reconciliation of all things with God at the end of time. It would seem that to contend the much smaller number of questionable verses pertaining to eternal punishment somehow establish it as an indisputable doctrine of the Christian faith requires that all of these other verses be explained away or overlooked, to say nothing of the history of the early Church and the preponderance of Church fathers who understood the Scriptures to teach something diametrically opposed to what became orthodox dogma in the 6th century.

One clever way St. Augustine attempted to explain away these Scriptures was by redefining the word "all" to not really mean **ALL** (such a simple word). Augustine said that *"all men"* did not mean *"all men without exception"*, but rather it meant *"some men from all classes of men without exclusion"*. Of course the problem with this contorted interpretation of "all men" is that it is selectively and inconsistently applied, even within the same verse of scripture! Take for example:

> *For as in Adam all die, so in Christ all will be made alive. (1 Cor 15:22)*

According to Christian doctrine, Adam's original sin resulted in **All people** being sentenced to mortal death. Given the inclusivity of "For as in Adam all die", does it pass the smell test that the Gospel author was meaning to exclude most people from "so in Christ all will be made alive"? I don't think so.

I don't know about you, but the dramatic and pervasive prevalence of "all", "all nations", "all people", "all men", "all creatures", "all things", etc. throughout both Old and New Testament scripture makes it somewhat difficult for me to believe *all* the different authors had the same understanding of the word "all" in mind when they wrote those verses. If we apply Augustine's definition of *all* to my last sentence, then only *some, but not all,* of the Bible authors would have concurred with Augustine's understanding of *all men.* So conversely, at least *some* of the New Testament authors would have meant *all men without exception* when they wrote their Scripture. So, Augustine's own argument would seem to disprove his very point.

Silly ... or profound? You be the judge.

Appendix A contains an extensive list of the verses in the Bible, both Old and New Testaments, that would appear to offer support for Universal Reconciliation. Enjoy.

"Recent" Church History

Now that we have discussed early Christian history at some length, let's quickly discuss the history of the Church and the path of Universal Reconciliation after its being declared anathema (heresy) in the 6th century. The ban on this more gracious view of God's nature, purpose and will coincided with the decline and disappearance of the Roman Empire in the 5th and 6th centuries. It marked the beginning of the 1000-year period of societal stagnation and collapse characterized by the control of the Church and the feudal system over life in Western Europe. This bleak and prolonged period has come to be called the Dark Ages.

Throughout the Dark Ages, the Church wielded extraordinary, and sometimes brutal, power and control over virtually every aspect of daily life. The Church and the clergy were self-acknowledged as God's sole representatives on earth. Feudal kings ruled by supposed divine right and usually with the support and approval of the Church. Conformance with Church doctrine and dictates was mandatory, with punishment by torture and sometimes death being meted out for heresy, and occasionally what might appear to have been even the most trivial infractions. The various Inquisitions (Medieval, Spanish, Portuguese and Roman) that began in the 12th century and lasted into the 19th century were the exclamation point on the Roman Church's power and control over the lives of its subjects.

During the Dark Ages and even into the early portion of the Protestant Reformation and Enlightenment Period that followed, the belief in Universal Reconciliation was persecuted to near extinction. However, a few brave souls managed to keep Universal Reconciliation barely alive, smoldering for centuries like embers in a dying campfire. A history of Universal Reconciliation during this period can be found at http://www.christianuniversalist.org/resources/articles/history-of-universalism/. So as not to unnecessarily add to the length of this book, I will allow the reader to read this account if they are so inclined.

After this long period of persecution and suppression, Universal Reconciliation began to reemerge from its long slumber. The impetus for this resurrection, even if it was a barely distinguishable reemergence at first, was nothing less than the Protestant Reformation itself.

"OK," you might be saying, "didn't the Reformation fix all the problems of the Roman Church and finally get Christianity and the Gospel message right?" That's a good question and one worth examining.

Martin Luther

The German monk, Martin Luther, is generally acknowledged as having launched the Reformation in 1517 when tradition has it that he nailed a copy of his *95 Theses* to the door of the Castle Church in Wittenberg, Germany. These theses contained a number of charges and accusations against the corrupt practices and errant beliefs of the Roman Church. Luther was particularly incensed at the sale of indulgences by the Church in which people were essentially extorted to purchase the forgiveness of the sins of their deceased loved ones to save them from the raging fires of hell. In addition to disagreeing with this and other Church practices, Luther also believed the Church had distorted the essential character of God and message of the Gospel. He maintained the Church had prevented people from a true understanding of these fundamental truths by excluding them from having access to the Bible, which the Church only allowed to be possessed or read by the clergy.

However, even though Martin Luther spawned the Reformation, he was no saint and there is ample reason to question whether he himself fully grasped Jesus' message of Good News, and command to love and forgive our fellow man. In spite of this, Luther was one of the first to come to the Protestant view that salvation from sin was solely through God's grace and as a result of faith alone in Jesus Christ. However, being apparently somewhat short on grace himself, Luther was virulently anti-Semitic, as were virtually all Christians of that time, viewing Jews as the "Christ killers". At one point Luther wrote, "We ought to take vengeance on the Jews and kill them!" However, not only did he advocate the killing of Jews, he also became incensed and inflamed toward the peasant class who used Luther's own rebellion against the Church to justify the Peasant Revolt against the king's divine right. In one of his works, Luther declared, "To kill a peasant is not murder; it is helping to extinguish the conflagration. Let there be no half measures! Crush them! Cut their throats! Transfix them! Leave no stone unturned! To kill a peasant is to destroy a mad dog."

Regarding these same Jews and peasants, one might ask, "What would Jesus do?" Or, WWJD in conservative Christian parlance. I think the answer is clear … not what Martin Luther advocated.

John Calvin

There's another key Reformation era figure worth discussing. Living at the same time as Martin Luther at the dawn of the Reformation, John Calvin was a French lawyer and also trained for the Catholic priesthood. He developed what came to be a widespread conservative Protestant doctrine known as Calvinism. Though originally from France, Calvin had to flee France for Basel, Switzerland, as a result of his heretical views against the Church. It was here he published his seminal work, *Institutes of the Christian Religion,* a systematic theology based upon the core premise that salvation is an act of God's grace attainable through faith alone in Jesus Christ, not works. Calvin ultimately came to lead the Reformed Church in Switzerland and his theology became the core doctrine of a number of different Protestant denominations, among them what became both the Presbyterian and Baptist denominations.

Calvin's doctrine is often referred to as the five points of Calvinism. The central tenets of his doctrine can be enumerated by the five-letter acronym, **TULIP**, which stands for:

Total depravity
Unconditional election
Limited atonement
Irresistible grace
Perseverance of the saints

In short, this means that as a result of Adam's original sin man is hopelessly lost in *total depravity.* Only those who accept God's son, Jesus Christ, in this life will receive the *limited attonement* of His *unconditional election* to salvation in His kingdom (i.e. heaven). Those who are so predestined for salvation will be called by God's *irresistible grace*. In addition, the salvation of God's *saints* will *persevere* forever (i.e. it cannot be lost).

One of the key notions in Calvin's soteriology (i.e. plan for salvation) is that God has predestined before the beginning of time a group of His *elect* for salvation. This limited salvation of only a small portion of God's children is rationalized by Calvinists as follows: Because all people are guilty of sin and therefore deserve God's eternal wrath, the salvation of anyone at all is asserted to be an exercise of His unconditional love and grace. In most respects, Calvin's theology is a direct extrapolation of Augustine's views and his redefinition of *"all men"* to mean *"all classes of men without exclusion"*, **NOT** *"all men without exception"*, which we have previously discussed.

Because of the severe exclusivity and arguably arbitrary selection by God of His elect, many people, including many Christians, have had problems with Calvin's view of God's love and grace. An alternative Protestant theology arose in opposition to Calvinism called Arminianism, named after the Dutch theologian Jacobus Arminius. In opposition to Calvinism, Arminianism asserted that Jesus died to save all sinners but whether or not a person would be saved depended upon his or her decision to accept or reject Christ. Many Christians found this view of God's love, mercy, justice and grace to be more palatable. Arminianism became the core theology of a number of other Protestant denominations including John Wesley's Methodist denomination, though many people contend Wesley himself came to believe in Universal Reconciliation later in life.

Like Martin Luther, there are good reasons to question whether John Calvin and his theology fully reflected the Good News and admonitions of Jesus to both love and forgive our enemies. A brief historical story will help shed light on why we might be concerned about this.

John Calvin and Miguel Servetus

Miguel Servetus was a Spanish physician and theologian who was a contemporary of John Calvin during the Reformation. As a physician, he is credited with having discovered the human circulatory system. Servetus was raised in a Spanish monastery and as a result had a keen interest in theology and the doctrinal issues central to the Reformation. He disagreed with Calvin on a number of points of Calvin's new "orthodox" reformed doctrine and wrote him a long letter describing his views and indicating he would like to travel to Geneva to meet and discuss these issues further. In a letter dated February 13, 1546, to his friend and colleague, William Farel, Calvin wrote:

> *"Servetus lately wrote to me and coupled with his letter a long volume of his delirious fancies, with the Thrasonic boast that I should see something astonishing and unheard of. He would like to come here [Geneva] if it is agreeable to me. But I do not want to pledge my word for his safety. For, if he comes, I will never let him depart alive, if I have any authority."*

Unfortunately, Servetus did make it to Geneva where he attended one of Calvin's sermons at which he was recognized and arrested by the local authorities at Calvin's direction. He was imprisoned, charged with heresy, tried, convicted and sentenced to death. He was subsequently burned alive over green wood taking more than three hours to die. John Calvin was instrumental in Servetus' arrest, trial and execution.

For many people, the above types of attitude and behavior by two of the most instrumental figures of the Protestant Reformation, Martin Luther and John Calvin, is troubling. It is directly at odds with Jesus' commandment for us to love and forgive our enemies. If they could rationalize the torture and murder of their enemies as authorized by the Bible, what might that say about the rest of their views on God's nature, purpose and will?

Answering the Arguments Against Universal Reconciliation

It is my contention that by denying the possibility of Universal Reconciliation, traditional and current orthodox Christian doctrine is in fact implicitly asserting that God does NOT unconditionally love. It is my firm conviction that a god who would punish one of his own children for all eternity **DOES NOT** unconditionally love that child. I believe this because any moral person would label an earthly father who excessively and brutally punishes one of his children a child abuser who does not love his children. Simply put, *love and excessive punishment are irreconcilable*. If that is true for an earthly father, must not God be a more perfect father than that? If hell is true, how do we reconcile the seeming contradiction between unconditional love and eternal punishment? Historical church tradition has come up with a number of explanations, most of which we have already addressed in detail within this book.

The denial of the perfection and universality of God's love is argued by the Orthodox Church along several lines. The following are the primary arguments made against God's plan to ultimately redeem all creation and all people, and brief answers to those arguments.

Argument 1: The Bible Clearly Teaches Hell and Eternal Punishment As the Fate of Those Who Do Not Accept Jesus in This Life

I believe most people who have taken the time to objectively read and study the information presented in this book, particularly those sections having to do with Biblical support **FOR** Universal Reconciliation, would acknowledge there is at least as much, *if not far more*, Biblical support for Universal Reconciliation as there is for the doctrines of hell and eternal punishment. IN ADDITION, in the majority of cases the natural meaning of those verses supporting Universal Reconciliation is clearer and less ambiguous than those claimed to support hell and eternal punishment, and not plagued with the Greek translation issues we have detailed elsewhere.

It is my belief that those who take the time to investigate these issues with an open mind and rigorous intellectual honesty (i.e. a sincere seeker of truth) will come to the conclusion that the Bible **DOES NOT** clearly and exclusively teach the traditional historical doctrines of hell and eternal punishment. Every person should sincerely test his or her faith by examining the information contained in this book with an open mind. Irrespective of where you ultimately come out on this issue, you will better know what the Bible says and your faith will be strengthened.

Argument 2: God May Be Love … But He Is Also Just and Must Exact Justice for Sin

The implication of this argument is that the only acceptable justice for rejecting God (and Jesus) in this life is eternal punishment in hell, **AND** this is the punishment that God demands! Though many Christians are not aware of it, this view has its modern roots in both St Augustine's 5th century teachings and St. Anselm's medieval explanation that the only acceptable punishment for sin against an infinite God is infinite punishment, but by accepting Jesus Christ in this life we accept his "free" gift of substitutionary atonement for our sins. This mantra has been repeated for so long and so often that most Christians accept it with little or no serious examination of the scriptural support, or lack thereof, that ostensibly teaches it.

As we have seen, there is voluminous scriptural support that appears to contradict this notion that God's justice *requires* eternal punishment. However, to be fair, if you impose a particular reading that, as we have shown elsewhere, is not in harmony with the vast majority of clear teachings by the original New Testament authors, a *very small* number of verses can be *alleged* to ostensibly support the notion.

> *However, there are NO Bible verses that unambiguously teach death as the end of the opportunity for salvation, or that it is incumbent upon God to impose eternal punishment for those not reconciled to Him by accepting Jesus Christ prior to their death.*

Conversely, there are a number of verses that indicate that death is not the end of God's love for all people and that He in fact defeats death and destroys it! So are we to believe that God will destroy death but torture forever the vast majority of His creation? Would it not have been more just, and certainly more humane, for God to allow those supposedly not destined for salvation to simply remain dead ... i.e., annihilated from His heavenly kingdom? What is just about His saving them from death only to subject them to eternal conscious torment? I ask you to search your heart, to ask the Holy Spirit, what kind of god does this? To believe such a thing, should we not be absolutely certain, and should it not be absolutely clear with no possibility of misunderstanding, that this is what the Bible says?

Most Christians accept the Biblical declaration in 1 John 4:8 and 16 that *"God is love"* as the most fundamental declaration of God's very *essence* or *nature*. He is not just loving ...
GOD IS LOVE!

Sadly some Christians, including the popular conservative Christian theologian J. I. Packer in his book *Knowing God*, diminish John's declaration concerning God. In his book, Packer states, *" 'God is love' is not the complete truth about God so far as the Bible is concerned ... [3 pages later] ... 'God is love' is the complete truth about God so far as the Christian is concerned."* The seeming implication of Packer's assertion is that God loves Christians but not the rest of mankind. Could it be possible that GOD IS LOVE but He doesn't love all people? If He doesn't love all people, how can we logically and rationally believe GOD IS LOVE? This is more than a little difficult to understand, and is the rocky shore upon which many would-be Christians have shipwrecked on their voyage of faith.

"God is love" is uniformly and identically translated in *every* major English Bible translation. There is no other such succinct declaration of God's nature in the Bible, in spite of many passages describing God's many and various *moral attributes* (e.g. just, merciful, forgiving, etc.). Specifically, there is no comparable declaration to *"God is love"* that describes His justice. Clearly God is just, but any objective reading of the Bible must acknowledge that *God's attribute of justice must necessarily be derived from and is an inextricable part of His very nature **as love***. In addition, as we have noted elsewhere, the Old Testament declaration *"His love endures forever"* is the single most frequently repeated phrase in the entire Bible.

In short, God is not love because He is just; He is just because He IS love.

Argument 3: If everyone is going to heaven anyway, why bother to obey God?

The principal focus of this question is the narrow understanding of salvation as simply going to heaven. As we have already noted in the section on salvation (*Are You Saved?*), Jesus spoke more about the kingdom of God being a spiritual realm available here and now than he did of it being an otherworldly future paradise. Salvation is as much about the process of personal transformation in which we willingly follow the example and teachings of Christ, and thereby find peace and joy in this life, *in addition to* realizing our future destiny in God's heavenly kingdom.

This question also assumes the prospect of spending eternity in hell is the strongest or only deterrent to living a life of sin and separation from God. If that is the case, this negative incentive has demonstrably and miserably failed at attracting people to Jesus Christ and God. The question also either diminishes or dismisses completely the role of self-inflicted (or divinely imposed?) suffering in this life or divinely administered punishment in the next in the process of our salvation. Contrary to the implications of this question, Universal Reconciliation explicitly affirms suffering AND punishment in this life AND beyond as the means by which God lovingly corrects and ultimately perfects us in preparation for citizenship in His eternal kingdom. Suffering and divine punishment administered *in love* are necessary prerequisites for the spiritual growth and transformation required for our ***voluntary*** repentance and embrace of God, and preparation for our spending eternity with Him. Is it any surprise that some might respond earlier and others later to God's efforts to woo us back to him? Even

Jesus declared that tax collectors and prostitutes would enter into God's kingdom *ahead of* (not in lieu of) the self-righteous scribes and Pharisees (Matt 21:32).

Argument 4: Do you mean that even someone like Hitler who killed so many millions of people will ultimately be restored to God's kingdom?

The short answer is yes. However, this question contains some interesting issues of incongruity and hypocrisy inter-mixed with a fundamental misunderstanding of the nature of sin and God's grace.

Let's first examine the absurd incongruity of this question. How is it possible that the question poses outrage at Hitler's brutal earthly murder of six million Jews, but is silent on the eternal conscious torture of these same tragic victims, and all other non-believers, at the hands of a "loving but just God"? I ask you in all sincerity to reflect on this incongruity by asking yourself the following question: **Is it morally consistent to condemn Hitler's atrocity as the depth of depravity, yet at the same time praise God's alleged eternal punishment of those who "die in sin" as being righteous and just?**

Are not both actions abhorrent to our moral compass ... the moral compass given us by God ... as well as God's own commandments to forgive? To further grasp the answer to this question, we must understand the nature of sin in the eyes of God and remind ourselves of God's mandate of forgiveness.

Most Christians would agree that sin is sin. There is no distinction between sins in God's eyes. As Paul so aptly wrote:

> *For all have sinned and fall short of the glory of God.*
> *(Rom 3:23)*

The implication of this is that whether a person has killed one person or six million, that person has sinned in the eyes of God. In addition, God's extension of mercy, forgiveness and grace to sinners is totally within His purview and sovereignty. And as we have discussed, His *justice* in punishing sin is derived from His nature as *love* (i.e. "God is love."), not vice versa.

The essence of this question implies that Hitler's sins were so great that it is hard to fathom how God could ever forgive him, as well as how totally repugnant his crimes are to our moral mind. When we confront this visceral reaction to such abhorrent sin, we must remember Jesus' words in the Sermon on the Mount:

> *"You have heard that it was said, 'Love your neigh-bor and hate your enemy.' But I tell you, love your enemies and pray for those who persecute you, that you may be children of your Father in heaven. He causes his sun to rise on the evil and the good, and sends rain on the righteous and the unrighteous. If you love those who love you, what reward will you get? Are not even the tax collectors doing that? And if you greet only your own people, what are you doing more than others? Do not even pagans do that? Be perfect, therefore, as your heavenly Father is perfect. (Matt 5:43-48)*

Is there any question what Jesus says we must do, **and what God does**, even if it is hard for our earthly human nature to imagine such magnanimous mercy and forgiveness? Truly we will only find and experience this kind of limitless grace in the spiritual kingdom and merciful arms of an infinite God who is love ... and do we not all require this unbounded kind of love, mercy, and forgiveness to redeem our own lives from the innu-merable sins we have committed?

Though it is human nature to count people's sins and hold them against them, it is God's nature to love, restore and forgive ... for His sake, not ours.

> Isa 43:25– "I, even I, am he who blots out your transgressions, for my own sake, and remembers your sins no more."

Argument 5: How could so many theologians be wrong about God, hell and eternal punishment?

As we discussed in the Prologue, the Church has an unfortunate history of misunderstanding the Bible and God on several significant moral and human rights issues. This should not be interpreted as a wholesale indictment of the Church or Christianity, only a statement of the flawed human nature of Church leadership at various points in history, including perhaps today. However, throughout the history of the Church there were also those brave saints who dared to challenge Church doctrines and teachings on certain issues that today we now understand were egregious mistakes made by the Church. These "heretics" changed the Church and Church doctrine for the better, and in keeping with a loving, merciful, forgiving and just God.

It is my contention that this is a similar moment in Christian history, when the authentic teachings of Jesus as recorded in the original Koine Greek will once and for all be clearly and accurately understood. Many theologians are letting their doctrinal predispositions encumber them with blinders that box them into patterns of repetitive, small thinking instead of taking a fresh look at the Bible in light of the best historical and linguistic understanding of the original Greek scriptures. A true understanding of the unconditional love and grace of God frees the human soul and spirit to respond to God out of love, not fear, and results in a dawning recognition that without a strong and abiding faith in such a God who is love and will one day redeem us all, God's creation would have no meaning ... to God or us! What would He have accomplished to create all of this, and then to lose the vast majority of His creation forever to sin and separation from Him? Would not the only thing worthy of an all-powerful God, and that would bring ultimate glory to Him, be for His love to win a *complete, consensual* victory over man's free will to reject Him and Jesus? If that is the greatest victory man can conceive for a God who is love, must not His victory be at least as great?

Conclusion

Dear brothers and sisters,

If you have made it to this point, you have covered much ground, explored new realms, and likely have sorely tested your faith. I sincerely appreciate your diligent effort and perseverance, and hope you have profoundly benefited from your journey.

Even more, I fervently hope you can begin to see just over the horizon ... to that time ... whether in this life or beyond ... when all hearts will, in their own time, freely turn to God and accept His perfect love, mercy, and forgiveness ... the profound mystery and gift of His unmerited grace. Like the father of the prodigal son, God does not and will not override our freedom to reject Him ... but patiently awaits ALL of His children's return to Him by their willful surrender to the unfathomable, perfect grace first taught and embodied by Jesus Christ. We will, all of us, one day turn purely as a result of His all-powerful, all-inclusive, unconditional love ... and the abiding mystery of His loving correction. Only when this time comes will God's creation once again be what He most longs for it to be … All in All.

> *"Love never fails … when perfection comes, the imperfect disappears."(1 Cor 13:8-10)*

Appendix A Universal Reconciliation Bible Verses

The following Bible verses are from the New International Version (either the 1984 or 2011 editions) and appear to support the notion of Universal Reconciliation either directly or indirectly.

Gen 12:3 – "... and all peoples on earth will be blessed through you."

Gen 18:18 – "All nations on earth will be blessed through him."

Gen 22:18 – "...through your offspring all nations on earth will be blessed"

Gen 26:4 – "...and through your offspring all nations on earth will be blessed"

Gen 28:14 – "All peoples on earth will be blessed through you and your offspring."

Deut 4:31 – "For the LORD your God is a merciful God; he will not abandon or destroy you ... "

2 Sam 14:14 – "Like water spilled on the ground, which cannot be recovered, so we must die. But God does not take away life; instead, he devises ways so that a banished person may not remain estranged from him."

Ps 22:27 –"All the ends of the earth will remember and turn to the LORD, and all the families of the nations will bow down before him,"

Ps 25:8 – "Good and upright is the LORD; therefore he instructs sinners in his ways."

Ps 30:5 – "For his anger lasts only a moment, but his favor lasts a lifetime;"

Ps 37:23-24 – "If the LORD delights in a man's way, he makes his steps firm; though he stumble, he will not fall, for the LORD upholds him with his hand."

Ps 62:1 – "My soul finds rest in God alone; my salvation comes from him."

Ps 65:2 – "O you who hear prayer, to you all people will come."

Ps 86:9 – "All the nations you have made will come and worship before you, O Lord; they will bring glory to your name."

Ps 103:8-9 – "The LORD is compassionate and gracious, slow to anger, abounding in love. He will not always accuse, nor will he harbor his anger forever;"

Ps 107:1 & 136:1 – "Give thanks to the LORD, for he is good; his love endures forever."

Ps 139:8 – "If I go up to the heavens, you are there; if I make my bed in the depths, you are there."

Ps 145:8-9 – "The LORD is gracious and compassionate, slow to anger and rich in love. The LORD is good to all; he has compassion on all he has made."

Ps 145:14 – "The LORD upholds all those who fall and lifts up all who are bowed down."

Ps 145:21 – "My mouth will speak in praise of the LORD. Let every creature praise his holy name for ever and ever."

Ecc 12:7 – "and the dust returns to the ground it came from, and the spirit returns to God who gave it."

Isa 4:4 – "The Lord will wash away the filth of the women of Zion; he will cleanse the bloodstains from Jerusalem by a spirit of judgment and a spirit of fire."

Isa 12:1-2 – "In that day you will say: 'I will praise you, O LORD. Although you were angry with me, your anger has turned away and you have comforted me. Surely God is my salvation; I will trust and not be afraid. The LORD, the LORD, is my strength and my song; he has become my salvation.'"

Isa 25:7-8 – "On this mountain he [God] will destroy the shroud that enfolds all peoples, the sheet that covers all nations; he will swallow up death forever. The Sovereign LORD will wipe away the tears from all faces; he will remove the disgrace of his people from all the earth."

Isa 40:5 – "And the glory of the Lord shall be revealed, and all flesh shall see it together, for the mouth of the Lord has spoken."

Isa 43:25 – "I, even I, am he who blots out your transgressions, for my own sake, and remembers your sins no more."

Isa 45:21-23 – "Declare what is to be, present it — let them take counsel together. Who foretold this long ago, who declared it from the distant past? Was it not

I, the LORD ? And there is no God apart from me, a righteous God and a Savior; there is none but me. Turn to me and be saved, all you ends of the earth; for I am God, and there is no other. By myself I have sworn, my mouth has uttered in all integrity a word that will not be revoked: Before me every knee will bow; by me every tongue will swear."

Isa 49:6 – "he says: 'It is too small a thing for you to be my servant to restore the tribes of Jacob and bring back those of Israel I have kept. I will also make you a light for the Gentiles, that you may bring my salvation to the ends of the earth.' "

Isa 49:14-15 – "But Zion said, 'The LORD has forsaken me, the Lord has forgotten me. Can a mother forget the baby at her breast and have no compassion on the child she has borne? Though she may forget, I will not forget you!'"

Isa 52:10 – "The LORD will lay bare his holy arm in the sight of all the nations, and all the ends of the earth will see the salvation of our God."

Isa 54:8 – "In a surge of anger I hid my face from you for a moment, but with everlasting kindness I will have compassion on you," says the LORD your Redeemer."

Isa 57:15-16–"For this is what the high and lofty One says—he who lives forever, whose name is holy: "I live in a high and holy place, but also with him who is contrite and lowly in spirit, to revive the spirit of the lowly and to revive the heart of the contrite. I will not accuse forever, nor will I always be angry, for then the spirit of man would grow faint before me—the breath of man that I have created."

Isa 66:18–"And I, because of their actions and their imaginations, am about to come and gather all nations and tongues, and they will come and see my glory."

Isa 66:23 – " '… all mankind will come and bow down before me,' says the LORD."

Jer 31:33-34–"This is the covenant I will make with the house of Israel after that time," declares the LORD. "I will put my law in their minds and write it on their hearts. I will be their God, and they will be my people. No longer will a man teach his neighbor, or a man his brother, saying, 'Know the LORD,' because they will all know me, from the least of them to the greatest," declares the LORD. "For I will forgive their wickedness and will remember their sins no more."

Lam 3:22 – "Because of the LORD's great love we are not consumed, for his compassions never fail."

Lam 3:31-33 – "For men are not cast off by the Lord forever. Though he brings grief, he will show compassion, so great is his unfailing love. For he does not willingly bring affliction or grief to the children of men."

Eze 16:53–"I will restore the fortunes of Sodom and her daughters and of Samaria and her daughters, and your fortunes along with them,"

Eze 36:26-27 – "I will give you a new heart and put a new spirit in you; I will remove from you your heart of stone and give you a heart of flesh. And I will put my Spirit in you"

Dan 9:9-10 – "The Lord our God is merciful and forgiving, even though we have rebelled against him; we have not obeyed the LORD our God or kept the laws he gave us through his servants the prophets."

Hos 11:9 – "I will not carry out my fierce anger, nor will I turn and devastate Ephraim. For I am God, and not man–the Holy One among you. I will not come in wrath."

Hos 13:14–"I will ransom them from the power of the grave; I will redeem them from death. Where, O death, are your plagues? Where, O grave, is your destruction? I will have no compassion,"

Joel 2:28-32:–"I will pour out my Spirit on all people. … And everyone who calls on the name of the Lord will be saved; … "

Mic 7:18 – "Who is a God like you, who pardons sin and forgives the transgression of the remnant of his inheritance? You do not stay angry forever but delight to show mercy."

Mal 2:10 – "Have we not all one Father? Did not one God create us?"

Matt 5:43-48 – "… But I tell you: Love your enemies and pray for those who persecute you, that you may be sons of your Father in heaven. He causes his sun to rise on the evil and the good, and sends rain on the righteous and the unrighteous. … Be perfect, therefore, as your heavenly Father is perfect."

Matt 11:28-30 – "Come to me, all you who are weary and burdened, and I will give you rest. Take my yoke upon you and learn from me, for I am gentle and humble in heart, and you will find rest for your souls. For my yoke is easy and my burden is light."

Matt 18:12-14 – "... If a man owns a hundred sheep, and one of them wanders away, will he not leave the ninety-nine on the hills and go to look for the one that wandered off? And if he finds it, I tell you the truth, he is happier about that one sheep than about the ninety-nine that did not wander off. In the same way your Father in heaven is not willing that any of these little ones should be lost."

Matt 19:23-26 – "... it is easier for a camel to go through the eye of a needle than for a rich man to enter the kingdom of God." When the disciples heard this, they ... asked, "Who then can be saved?" Jesus ... said, "With man this is impossible, but with God all things are possible."

Matt 20:1-15 – Jesus' parable of the land owner and the workers in the field. The owner (God) rewards those who come last the same as those who came first.

Mark 3:28 – "I tell you the truth, all the sins and blasphemies of men will be forgiven them."

Luke 2:10 – "But the angel said to them, 'Do not be afraid. I bring you good news of great joy that will be for all the people.' "

Luke 2:30-32 – "For my eyes have seen your salvation, which you have prepared in the sight of all people, a light for revelation to the Gentiles and for glory to your people Israel."

Luke 3:6 – "All mankind will see God's salvation."

Luke 6:35-36 – "But love your enemies, do good to them, and lend to them without expecting to get anything back. Then your reward will be great, and you will be sons of the Most High, because he is kind to the ungrateful and wicked. Be merciful, just as your Father is merciful.

Luke 15:4-7 – "Suppose one of you has a hundred sheep and loses one of them. Does he not leave the ninety-nine in the open country and go after the lost sheep until he finds it? ... I tell you that in the same way there will be more rejoicing in heaven over one sinner who repents than over ninety-nine righteous persons who do not need to repent. "

Luke 15:8-9 – "Or suppose a woman has ten silver coins and loses one. Does she not light a lamp, sweep the house and search carefully until she finds it? And when she finds it, she calls her friends and neighbors together and says, 'Rejoice with me; I have found my lost coin.' "

Luke 15:11-32 – Jesus' parable of the prodigal son. The father waits until his lost son finally returns home and throws a big celebration upon his return. The older brother who had remained home working for his father becomes jealous and angry. His faithfulness to his father was not sincere, and he expected more than his lost brother who returned. Now the father must and will wait for the older brother to repent and return. This parable is about God's patience and grace.

Luke 19:10 – "The Son of Man came to seek and save what was lost."

Luke 20:38 – "He is not the God of the dead, but of the living, for to him all are alive."

Luke 23:34 – "Jesus said, 'Father, forgive them, for they do not know what they are doing.'"

John 1:29 – "The next day John saw Jesus coming toward him and said, "Look, the Lamb of God, who takes away the sin of the world!"

John 3:17 – "For God did not send his Son into the world to condemn the world, but to save the world through him."

John 4:42 – "They said to the woman, "We no longer believe just because of what you said; now we have heard for ourselves, and we know that this man really is the Savior of the world."

John 6:37-39 – "All that the Father gives me will come to me, and whoever comes to me I will never drive away. For I have come down from heaven not to do my will but to do the will of him who sent me. And this is the will of him who sent me, that I shall lose none of all that he has given me, but raise them up at the last day."

John 6:45 – "It is written in the Prophets: 'They will all be taught by God.' Everyone who listens to the Father and learns from him comes to me."

John 5:22 – "Moreover, the Father judges no one, but has entrusted all judgment to the Son,"

John 8:15 – "You judge by human standards; I pass judgment on no one."

John 10:14-16 – "I am the good shepherd; I know my sheep and my sheep know me — just as the Father knows me and I know the Father — and I lay down my life for the sheep. I have other sheep that are not of this sheep pen. I must bring them also. They too will listen to my voice, and there shall be one flock and one shepherd."

John 12:32 – "But I, when I am lifted up from the earth, I will draw all people to myself."

John 12:46-47–46I have come into the world as a light, so that no one who believes in me should stay in darkness. As for the person who hears my words but does not keep them, I do not judge him. For I did not come to judge the world, but to save it."

John 17:1-2 – "Father, the time has come. Glorify your Son, that your Son may glorify you. For you granted him authority over all people that he might give eternal life to all those you have given him."

Acts 3:20-21 – " … and that he may send the Christ, who has been appointed for you — even Jesus. He must remain in heaven until the time comes for God to restore everything, as he promised long ago through his holy prophets."

Acts 3:25-26 – "And you are heirs of the prophets and of the covenant God made with your fathers. He said to Abraham, 'Through your offspring all peoples on earth will be blessed.' When God raised up his servant, he sent him first to you to bless you by turning each of you from your wicked ways."

Acts 13:47 – "For this is what the Lord has commanded us: " 'I have made you a light for the Gentiles, that you may bring salvation to the ends of the earth.' "

Acts 24:14-15 – "However, I admit that I worship the God of our fathers as a follower of the Way, which they call a sect. I believe everything that agrees with the Law and that is written in the Prophets, and I have the same hope in God as these men, that there will be a resurrection of both the righteous and the wicked." [Said by Paul at his trial before Felix, governor of Caesarea]

Rom 5:6-8 – "You see, at just the right time, when we were still powerless, Christ died for the ungodly. Very rarely will anyone die for a righteous man, though for a good man someone might possibly dare to die. But God demonstrates his own love for us in this: While we were still sinners, Christ died for us."

Rom 5:18 – "just as the result of one trespass was condemnation for all people, so also the result of one act of righteousness was justification that brings life for all people."

Rom 6:14 – "For sin shall not be your master, because you are not under law, but under grace."

Rom 6:23 – "For the wages of sin is death, but the gift of God is eternal life in Christ Jesus our Lord."

Rom 8:19-23 – "The creation waits in eager expectation for the sons of God to be revealed. For the creation was subjected to frustration, not by its own choice, but by the will of the one who subjected it, in hope that the creation itself will be liberated from its bondage to decay and brought into the glorious freedom of the children of God. We know that the whole creation has been groaning as in the pains of childbirth right up to the present time. Not only so, but we ourselves, who have the first fruits of the Spirit, groan inwardly as we wait eagerly for our adoption as sons, the redemption of our bodies."

Rom 8:38-39 – "For I am convinced that neither death nor life, neither angels nor demons, neither the present nor the future, nor any powers, neither height nor depth, nor anything else in all creation, will be able to separate us from the love of God that is in Christ Jesus our Lord."

Rom 11:25-32 – "I do not want you to be ignorant of this mystery, brothers, so that you may not be conceited: Israel has experienced a hardening in part until the full number of the Gentiles has come in. And so all Israel will be saved, as it is written:
'The deliverer will come from Zion;
he will turn godlessness away from Jacob.
And this is my covenant with them when I take away their sins.'

As far as the gospel is concerned, they are enemies on your account; but as far as election is concerned, they are loved on account of the patriarchs [i.e. the Jews are also God's "elect"], for God's gifts and his call are irrevocable. Just as you who were at one time disobedient to God have now received mercy as a result of their disobedience, so they too have now become disobedient in order that they too may now receive mercy as a result of God's mercy to you. For God has bound everyone over to disobedience so that he may have mercy on them all."

Rom 14:7-8 – "For none of us lives to himself alone and none of us dies to himself alone. If we live, we live to the Lord; and if we die, we die to the Lord. So, whether we live or die, we belong to the Lord."

Rom 14:11 – "It is written: 'As surely as I live,' says the Lord, 'every knee will bow before me; every tongue will confess to God.' "

1 Cor 13:8-10 – "Love never fails … when perfection comes, the imperfect disappears."

1 Cor 15:20-28 – "For as in Adam all die, so in Christ all will be made alive. But each in his own turn: Christ, the first fruits; then, when he comes, those who belong to him. Then the end will come, when he hands over the kingdom to God the Father after he has destroyed all dominion, authority and power. For he must reign until he has put all his enemies under his feet. The last enemy to be destroyed is death. For he "has put everything under his feet." Now when it says that "everything" has been put under him, it is clear that this does not include God himself, who put everything under Christ. When he has done this, then the Son himself will be made subject to him who put everything under him, so that God may be all in all." [All of God's creation will have been restored to Him.]

1 Cor 15:42-55 – "So will it be with the resurrection of the dead. The body that is sown is perishable, it is raised imperishable; it is sown in dishonor, it is raised in glory; it is sown in weakness, it is raised in power; it is sown a natural body, it is raised a spiritual body. If there is a natural body, there is also a spiritual body. So it is written: "The first man Adam became a living being"; the last Adam, a life-giving spirit. The spiritual did not come first, but the natural, and after that the spiritual. The first man was of the dust of the earth, the second man from heaven. As was the earthly man, so are those who are of the earth;

and as is the man from heaven, so also are those who are of heaven. And just as we have borne the likeness of the earthly man, so shall we bear the likeness of the man from heaven. I declare to you, brothers, that flesh and blood cannot inherit the kingdom of God, nor does the perishable inherit the imperishable. Listen, I tell you a mystery: We will not all sleep, but we will all be changed— in a flash, in the twinkling of an eye, at the last trumpet. For the trumpet will sound, the dead will be raised imperishable, and we will be changed. For the perishable must clothe itself with the imperishable, and the mortal with immortality. When the perishable has been clothed with the imperishable, and the mortal with immortality, then the saying that is written will come true: "Death has been swallowed up in victory. Where, O death, is your victory? Where, O death, is your sting?"

2 Cor 3:9-11 – "If the ministry that condemns men is glorious, how much more glorious is the ministry that brings righteousness! For what was glorious has no glory now in comparison with the surpassing glory. And if what was fading away came with glory, how much greater is the glory of that which lasts!"

2 Cor 3:18 – "And we, who with unveiled faces all reflect the Lord's glory, are being transformed into his likeness with ever-increasing glory, which comes from the Lord, who is the Spirit."

2 Cor 5:14 – "For Christ's love compels us, because we are convinced that one died for all, and therefore all died."

2 Cor 5:18-19 – "All this is from God, who reconciled us to himself through Christ and gave us the ministry of reconciliation: that God was reconciling the world to himself in Christ, not counting men's sins against them. And he has committed to us the message of reconciliation."

Gal 3:8 – "The Scripture foresaw that God would justify the Gentiles by faith, and announced the gospel in advance to Abraham: "All nations will be blessed through you.""

Eph 1:9-10 – "And he made known to us the mystery of his will according to his good pleasure, which he purposed in Christ, to be put into effect when the times will have reached their fulfillment —to bring all things in heaven and on earth together under one head, even Christ."

Eph 2:1-9 – "As for you, you were dead in your transgressions and sins, in which you used to live when you followed the ways of this world and of the ruler of the kingdom of the air, the spirit who is now at work in those who are disobedient. All of us also lived among them at one time, gratifying the cravings of our sinful nature and following its desires and thoughts. Like the rest, we were by nature objects of wrath. But because of his great love for us, God, who is rich in mercy, made us alive with Christ even when we were dead in transgressions—it is by grace you have been saved. And God raised us up with Christ and seated us with him in the heavenly realms in Christ Jesus, in order that in the coming ages he might show the incomparable riches of his grace, expressed in his kindness to us in Christ Jesus. For it is by grace you have been saved, through faith—and this not from yourselves, it is the gift of God— not by works, so that no one can boast."

Phil 2:9-11 – "Therefore God exalted him to the highest place and gave him the name that is above every name, that at the name of Jesus every knee should bow, in heaven and on earth and under the earth, and every tongue confess that Jesus Christ is Lord, to the glory of God the Father."

Phil 3:20-21 – "But our citizenship is in heaven. And we eagerly await a Savior from there, the Lord Jesus Christ, who, by the power that enables him to bring everything under his control, will transform our lowly bodies so that they will be like his glorious body."

Col 1:15-23 – "He [Christ] is the image of the invisible God, the firstborn over all creation. For by him all things were created: things in heaven and on earth, visible and invisible, whether thrones or powers or rulers or authorities; all things were created by him and for him. He is before all things, and in him all things hold together. And he is the head of the body, the church; he is the beginning and the firstborn from among the dead, so that in everything he might have the supremacy. For God was pleased to have all his fullness dwell in him, and through him to reconcile to himself all things, whether things on earth or things in heaven, by making peace through his blood, shed on the cross. Once you were alienated from God and were enemies in your minds because of your evil behavior. But now he has reconciled you by Christ's physical body through death to present you holy in his sight, without blemish and free from accusation — if you continue in your faith, established and firm, not moved from the hope held out in the gospel. This is the gospel that you heard and that has been proclaimed to every creature under heaven, and of which I, Paul, have become a servant.

1 Tim 2:1-6 – "I urge, then, first of all, that requests, prayers, intercession and thanksgiving be made for everyone — for kings and all those in authority, that we may live peaceful and quiet lives in all godliness and holiness. This is good, and pleases God our Savior, who wants all people to be saved and to come to a knowledge of the truth. For there is one God and one mediator between God and men, the man Christ Jesus, who gave himself as a ransom for all people — the testimony given in its proper time."

1 Tim 4:9-10 – "This is a trustworthy saying that deserves full acceptance (and for this we labor and strive), that we have put our hope in the living God, who is the Savior of all people, and especially of those who believe."

Titus 2:11 – "For the grace of God that brings salvation has appeared to all people."

Titus 3:4-7 – "But when the kindness and love of God our Savior appeared, he saved us, not because of righteous things we had done, but because of his mercy. He saved us through the washing of rebirth and renewal by the Holy Spirit, whom he poured out on us generously through Jesus Christ our Savior, so that, having been justified by his grace, we might become heirs having the hope of eternal life."

Heb 2:9 – "But we see Jesus, who was made a little lower than the angels, now crowned with glory and honor because he suffered death, so that by the grace of God he might taste death for everyone."

Heb 2:14-15 – "Since the children have flesh and blood, he too shared in their humanity so that by his death he might destroy him who holds the power of death — that is, the devil — and free those who all their lives were held in slavery by their fear of death."

Heb 8:10-12 – "This is the covenant I will make with the house of Israel after that time, declares the Lord. I will put my laws in their minds and write them on their hearts. I will be their God, and they will be my people. No longer will a man teach his neighbor, or a man his brother, saying, 'Know the Lord, because they will all know me, from the least of them to the greatest. For I will forgive their wickedness and will remember their sins no more."

Heb 10:15-17 – "The Holy Spirit also testifies to us about this. First he says: 'This is the covenant I will make with them after that time, says the Lord. I will put my laws in their hearts, and I will write them on their minds.' Then he adds: 'Their sins and lawless acts I will remember no more.'"

2 Pet 3:9 – "The Lord is not slow in keeping his promise, as some understand slowness. He is patient with you, not wanting anyone to perish, but everyone to come to repentance."

1 John 2:2 – "He is the atoning sacrifice for our sins, and not only for ours but also for the sins of the whole world."

1 John 3:19-20 – "This then is how we know that we belong to the truth, and how we set our hearts at rest in his presence whenever our hearts condemn us. For God is greater than our hearts, and he knows everything."

1 John 4:7-11 – "Dear friends, let us love one another, for love comes from God. Everyone who loves has been born of God and knows God. Whoever does not love does not know God, because God is love. This is how God showed his love among us: He sent his one and only Son into the world that we might live through him. This is love: not that we loved God, but that he loved us and sent his Son as an atoning sacrifice for our sins. Dear friends, since God so loved us, we also ought to love one another."

1 John 4:14 – "And we have seen and testify that the Father has sent his Son to be the Savior of the world."

1 John 4:16 – "And so we know and rely on the love God has for us. God is love. Whoever lives in love lives in God, and God in him."

1 John 4:19 – "We love because he first loved us."

Rev 5:13 – "Then I heard every creature in heaven and on earth and under the earth and on the sea, and all that is in them, singing: "To him who sits on the throne and to the Lamb be praise and honor and glory and power, for ever and ever!"

Rev 15:4 – "Who will not fear you, O Lord, and bring glory to your name? For you alone are holy. All nations will come and worship before you, for your righteous acts have been revealed."

Rev 21:1-5 – "Then I saw a new heaven and a new earth, for the first heaven and the first earth had passed away, and there was no longer any sea. I saw the Holy City, the new Jerusalem, coming down out of heaven from God, prepared as a bride beautifully dressed for her husband. And I heard a loud voice from the throne saying, 'Now the dwelling of God is with men, and he will live with them. They will be his people, and God himself will be with them and be their God. He will wipe every tear from their eyes. There will be no more death or mourning or crying or pain, for the old order of things has passed away.' He who was seated on the throne said, 'I am making everything new!' Then he said, 'Write this down, for these words are trustworthy and true.'"

Rev 22:2 – "down the middle of the great street of the city. On each side of the river stood the tree of life, bearing twelve crops of fruit, yielding its fruit every month. And the leaves of the tree are for the healing of the nations."

Rev 22:17 – "The Spirit and the bride say, 'Come!' And let him who hears say, 'Come!' Whoever is thirsty, let him come; and whoever wishes, let him take the free gift of the water of life."

Appendix B Early Church Fathers

The following is a list of early Church fathers whose writings indicate that they believed in Universal Reconciliation. The link associated with the father's name is to the official Catholic Church Encyclopedia entry at www.newadvent.org. The link associated with the father's timeframe in the early Church is to the Wikipedia reference. Due to differences among different reference sources, all dates are given as approximate.

St. Irenaeus, Bishop of Lyons (c. 130-200 AD)

St. Pantaenus, 1st head of Didascaleion (c. 180 AD)

St. Clement of Alexandria (c. 150-215 AD)

Origen (c. 185-254 AD)

Theophilus of Antioch (c. 168 AD)

St. Addai, 1st Bishop of Edessa (c. late 2nd century AD)

St. Gregory Thaumaturgus (c. 213-270 AD)

St. Pamphilus of Caesarea (d. 309 AD)

Eusebius of Caesarea (c. 260-341 AD)

St. Athanasius, "The Father of Orthodoxy" (c. 296-373 AD)

Didymus the Blind (c. 309-395 AD)

Diodore of Tarsus (d. 392 AD)

St. Macrina the Younger (c. 327-379 AD)

St. Basil the Great, Bishop of Caesarea (c. 329-379 AD)

St. Gregory of Nazianzus, Bishop of Constantinople (c. 330-390 AD)

St. Gregory of Nyssa, leading theologian of Eastern Church (c. 332-398 AD)

St. Ambrose, Bishop of Milan (c. 340-397 AD)

St. Jerome (c. 342-420 AD), created Latin Vulgate

St. John Chrysostom (c. 347-407 AD)

Theodore of Mopsuestia (c. 350-428 AD)

Theodoret the Blessed, Bishop of Cyrrhus (c. 393-457 AD)

St. Hilary, Bishop of Poitiers (d. 363 AD)

Titus, Bishop of Bostra (b. 362-371 AD)

St. Cyril of Alexandria (c. 376-444 AD)

St. Peter Chrysologus, Bishop of Ravenna (c. 406-450 AD)

St. Maximus of Turin(c. 380-465 AD)

Olympiodorus, philosophical opposer of Justinian (c. 550 AD)

Quotes of the Early Church Fathers

The following quotes are from the writings of the early Church fathers to which the quote is attributed.

> *"But we maintain, that the power of Christ's cross and of his death … is so great, that it will be sufficient for the healing and restoration of not only the present and future ages, but even for those of the past."–Origen (185-254 AD),"The Father of Theology"*

> *"Wherefore also He drove him (Adam) out of Paradise, and removed him far from the tree of life, not because He envied him the tree of life, as some dare to assert, but because He pitied him and desired that he should not continue always a sinner, and that the sin which surrounded him should not be immortal,*

and the evil interminable and irremediable." – St. Irenaeus, Bishop of Lyons

"… yet we hold that in the mind there is no evil so strong that it may not be overcome by the Supreme Word and God. For stronger than all the evils in the soul is the Word, and the healing power that swells in Him, and the healing He applies, according to the will of God to every man. The consummation of all things is the destruction of evil … " – Origen

"For that for which our Lord came into the world was altogether to teach and show that at the end of created things is a resurrection for all men. And at that time their acts of conduct will be represented on their own persons, and their bodies become volumes for the written things of justice, and there will not be he who knoweth not writing; because that every man shall read the letters of his own book at that day, and the account of his actions he taketh with the fingers of his hands." – The Doctrine of Addai (c. late 2nd century – early 3rd century)

"Mankind, being reclaimed from their sins … are to be subjected to Christ in the fullness of the dispensation instituted for the salvation of all." and "In the liberation of all no one remains a captive! At the time of the Lord's passion the devil alone was injured by losing all of the captives he was keeping." – Didymus the Blind

"And God showed great kindness to man, in this, that He did not suffer him to continue being in sin forever; but as it were, by a kind of banishment, cast him out of paradise in order that, having punishment expiated within an appointed time, and having been

disciplined, he should afterwards be recalled…just as a vessel, when one being fashioned it has some flaw, is remolded or remade that it may become new and entire; so also it happens to man by death. For he is broken up by force, that in the resurrection he may be found whole; I mean spotless, righteous and immortal." – Theophilus of Antioch

"The wicked who have committed evil the whole period of their lives shall be punished till they learn that, by continuing in sin, they only continue in misery. And when, by this means, they shall have been brought to fear God, and to regard Him with good will, they shall obtain the enjoyment of His grace." – Theodore of Mopsuestia

"In the present life God is in all, for his nature is without limits, but is not all in all. But in the coming life, when mortality is at an end and immortality granted, and sin has no longer any place, God will be all in all. For the Lord, who loves man, punishes medicinally, that he may check the course of impiety." –Theodoret the Blessed

"Our Lord is the One who delivers man [all people], and who heals the inventor of evil himself [Satan]." and "For it is needful that evil should some day be wholly and absolutely removed out of the circle of being." – St. Gregory of Nyssa, Bishop of Nyssa

"Abyss of hell is, indeed, the place of torment; but it is not eternal, nor did it exist in the original constitution of nature. It was made afterward, as a remedy for sinners, that it might cure them. And the punishments are holy, as they are remedial and salutary in their effect on transgressors; for they are inflicted

not to preserve them in their wickedness but to make them cease from their wickedness. The anguish of their suffering compels them to break off their vices." – Titus, Bishop of Bostra

"For the wicked are punished, not perpetual, but they are to be tormented for a certain brief period … according to the amount of malice in their works. They shall therefore suffer punishment for a short space, but immortal blessedness, having no end awaits them. The resurrection, therefore is regarded as a blessing not only to the good but also to the evil." – Diodore of Tarsus, Bishop of Tarsus and Jerusalem

"The whole human race lost in Adam, followed the one [Christ], seeks the one in order that in the one he may restore all." – St. Peter Chrysologus, Bishop of Ravenna

"These, if they will, may go Christ's way, but if not let them go their way. In another place perhaps they shall be baptized with fire, that last baptism, which is not only painful, but enduring also; which eats up, as if it were hay, all defiled matter, and consumes all vanity and vice." – St. Gregory of Nazianzus, Bishop of Constantinople

"The Lord descends to the infernal world, in order that even those, who were in the infernal abodes, should be set free from their perpetual bonds." – St. Ambrose, Bishop of Milan

"While the devil imagined that he got hold of Christ, he really lost all of those he was keeping." – St. John Chrysostom, Doctor of the Greek Church

"He shews the reason of penalty, for the Lord, who loves men, chastises in order to heal, like a physician,

that He may arrest the course of our sin." – *Theodoret the Blessed , Bishop of Cyrrhus*

Describing Christ as having emptied Hades, and "left the devil there solitary and deserted." – *St. Cyril of Alexandria*

"The Word seems to me to lay down the doctrine of the perfect obliteration of wickedness, for if God shall be in all things that are, obviously wickedness shall not be in them. For it is necessary that at some time evil should be removed utterly and entirely from the realm of being." – *St. Macrina the Younger*

"The whole human race, who are one, are the one lost sheep, which is destined to be found by the Good Shepherd." – *St. Hilary, Archbishop of Poitiers*

"We can set no limits to the agency of the Redeemer to redeem, to rescue, to discipline in his work, and so will he continue to operate after this life." and *"All men are Christ's, some by knowing Him, the rest not yet. He is the Savior, not of some and the rest not. For how is He Savior and Lord, if not the Savior and Lord of all?"* – *St. Clement of Alexandria*

"The Son 'breaking in pieces' His enemies is for the sake of remolding them, as a potter his own work; as Jeremiah 18:6 says: i.e., to restore them once again to their former state." – *Eusebius of Caesarea, Bishop of Caesarea*

"Our Savior has appointed two kinds of resurrection in the Apocalypse. 'Blessed is he that hath part in the first resurrection,' for such come to grace without the judgment. As for those who do not come to the first, but are reserved unto the second resurrection, these shall be disciplined until their appointed times,

between the first and the second resurrection." – St. Ambrose, Bishop of Milan

"In the present life God is in all, for His nature is without limits, but he is not all in all. But in the coming life, when mortality is at an end and immortality granted, and sin has no longer any place, God will be all in all. For the Lord, who loves man, punishes medicinally, that He may check the course of impiety." – Theodoret the Blessed

"In the end and consummation of the Universe all are to be restored into their original harmonious state, and we all shall be made of one body and be united once more into a perfect man, and the prayer of our Savior shall be fulfilled that all may be one." – St. Jerome, author of Latin Vulgate Bible

"The nations are gathered to the Judgment, that on them may be poured out the wrath of the fury of the Lord, and this in pity and with a design to heal in order that every one may return to the confession of the Lord, that in Jesus' Name every knee may bow, and every tongue may confess that He is Lord. All God's enemies shall perish, not that they cease to exist, but cease to be enemies." – St. Jerome

"Do not suppose that the soul is punished for endless aions in Tartarus. Very properly, the soul is not punished to gratify the revenge of the divinity, but for the sake of healing. But we say the soul is punished for an aionion period, calling its life, and its allotted period of punishment, its aion." – Olympiodorus, philosophical antagonist of Justinian

"The Lord's peace is co-extensive with all time. For all things shall be subject to him, and all things shall *acknowledge his empire; and when God shall be all in all, those who now excite discord by revolts having been pacified, shall praise God in peaceful concord."–* St. Basil the Great, Bishop of Caesarea

"While the devil thought to kill One [Christ], he is deprived of all those cast out of hades, and he [the devil] sitting by the gates, sees all fettered beings led forth by the courage of the Saviour." – St. Athanasius, the Great "Father of Orthodoxy"

"Christ carried off to heaven man (mankind) whose cause He undertook, snatched from the jaws of Hades." – St. Maximus of Turin

References

1. Aiken, Mercy and Amirault, Gary, "The Case Against Hell", http://www.tentmaker.org/articles/ifhellisreal. htm, May 2006
2. Allen, Ken, Christian Universalism Articles
3. Allin, Thomas and Chamberlain, Mark T., Every Knee Shall Bow, (Xulon Press, 2005)
4. Allin, Thomas, Christ Triumphant, (Canyon Country, CA: Concordant Publishing Concern, 9th edition, 1st edition originally published 1895), accessed at http://www.tentmaker.org/books/ChristTriumphant.htm, June 2006
5. Amirault, Gary, "Bible Translations That Do Not Teach Eternal Torment, http://www.tentmaker.org/books/GatesOfHell.html, May 2006
6. Amirault, Gary, "The Early Christian View of the Savior", http://www.tentmaker.org/books/EarlyChristianView.html, May 2006
7. Beauchemin, Gerry, Hope Beyond Hell (Olmito, TX: Malista Press, 2007), accessed at http://www.hopebeyondhell.net///Revised_Edition.pdf
8. Beecher, Edward, D.D., History of Opinions On The Scriptural Doctrine of Retribution, (New York, NY: D. Appleton & Co., 1878), accessed at http://www.

tentmaker.org/books/Retribution/DoctrineOfRetribu-
tion.html

9. BibleGateway, www.BibleGateway.com, May 2006

10. Bonda, Jan, The One Purpose of God, (Grand Rapids, MI: Wm. B. Eerdsman Publishing Co., 1998)

11. Buxtorf, Johannes, Synagoga Judaica (Juden-schül), translated by Alan D. Corré, accessed at http://www.uwm.edu/~corre/buxdorf/index.html, June 2006

12. Catholic Encyclopedia, www.NewAdvent.org, May 2006

13. Coptic Orthodox Church Network, www.coptic-church.net, May 2006

14. Ehrman, Bart D., Misquoting Jesus, The Story Behind Who Changed the Bible and Why, (New York, NY: HarperCollins Publishers, Inc., 2005)

15. Friedman, Richard Elliot, Who Wrote The Bible?, (NY, NY: HarperCollins Publishers, 1987)

16. Gulley, Philip and Mulholland, James, If Grace is True: Why God Will Save Every Person, (New York, NY: HarperCollins Publishers, 2003)

17. Hanson, John Wesley, D.D., Bible Proofs of Universal Salvation, (Chicago, IL: Hansen, J.W., 1877)

18. Hanson, John Wesley, D.D., The Greek Word Aion-Aionios Translated Everlasting—Eternal in the Holy Bible, (Chicago, IL; Northwest Universalist Publishing House, 1875)

19. Hanson, John Wesley, D.D., Aion-Aionios:An Excursus on the Greek Word Rendered Everlasting, Eternal, Etc., in the Holy Bible (Chicago, IL; Jansen, McClurg, & Company, 1880)

20. Hanson, John Wesley, D.D., The Bible Hell (Boston, MA; Universalist Publishing House, 1888)

21. Hanson, John Wesley, D.D., Universalism: The Prevailing Doctrine Of The Christian Church During Its First Five Hundred Years, (Boston, MA and Chicago, IL: Universalist Publishing House, 1899

22. Holy Bible: King James Version, accessed via www.BibleGateway.com, May 2006

23. Holy Bible: New International Version, (Grand Rapids, MI: Zondervan Publishing House, 1984), accessed via www.BibleGateway.com, May 2006

24. Holy Bible: New King James Version, accessed via www.BibleGateway.com, May 2006

25. Holy Bible: Today's New International Version, (Grand Rapids, MI: Zondervan Publishing House, 2003), accessed via http://www.tniv.info, July 2006

26. Holy Bible: Young's Literal Translation, accessed via www.BibleGateway.com, May 2006

27. Hough, Dean, "Concerning Aion and Aionios", http://www.concordant.org/expohtml/TheEons/aion.html

28. Jukes, Rev. Andrew, The Second Death and the Restitution of All Things, (Santa Clarita, CA: Concordant Publishing Concern, republished 2001), accessed at http://www.hopebeyondhell.net/page5.html

29. MacDonald, Gregory, The Evangelical Universalist, (Eugene, OR: Wipf & Stock, 2006)

30. Manford, Erasmus, "One Hundred and Fifty Reasons for Believing in the Final Salvation of All Mankind", http://www.tentmaker.org/books/150reasons.html, May 2006

31. Martin, Ernest, Ph.D., "The Real Meaning of the Rich Man and Lazarus", http://www.what-the-hell-is-hell.com/HellArticles/RichManParable.htm, May 2006

32. NewAdvent, "Origen and Origenism", http://www.newadvent.org/cathen/11306b.htm, May 2006

33. Nungesser, Tony and Amirault, Gary, " 'Eternal' Punishment (Matthew 25:46) is NOT Found in the The Greek New Testament", http://www.tentmaker.org/articles/EternalPunishmentNotTrueToGreek.html

34. Packer, J. I., Knowing God, (Intervarsity Press, 1993)

35. Pearson, Carlton, The Gospel of Inclusion, (AZUSA Press International, 2006)

36. Stevenson, G.T., Time and Eternity: A Biblical Study, accessed at http://www.tentmaker.org/books/time/index.html

37. Talbott, Thomas, The Inescapable Love of God, (Universal Publishers, 1999; reprint, 2002)

38. Vincent, Ken R., The Golden Thread, (Lincoln, NE: iUniverse, 2005)

39. Taylor, Larry, "Calvinism vs. Arminianism", http://www.ccfestus.com/books/taylor_calvinism.htm, May 2006

40. Tentmaker Ministries, www.tentmaker.org, May 2006

41. Tentmaker Ministries, "Universalism is Not in the Bible", http://www.tentmaker.org/articles/universalism-is-not-in-the-bible.htm, May 2006

42. Tompkins, Stephen, A Short History of Christianity, (Oxford, England: Lion Hudson plc, 2005)

43. Thayer, Thomas B., The Origin and History of the Doctrine of Endless Punishment, (Boston, MA: Universalist Publishing House, 1855), accessed at http://www.tentmaker.org/books/OriginandHistory.html

44. The Internet Encyclopedia of Philosophy, http://www.iep.utm.edu/, May 2006

45. The Bible Museum, Inc., "English Bible History", http://www.greatsite.com/timeline-english-bible-history/, May 2006

46. The Stanford Encyclopedia of Philosophy, http://plato.stanford.edu/entries/eternity

47. Watson, David Lowes, God Does Not Foreclose; The Universal Promise of Salvation (Nashville, TN: Abingdon, Press, 1990)

48. Wiener, Peter, Martin Luther: Hitler's Spiritual Ancestor, http://www.tentmaker.org/books/MartinLuther-HitlersSpiritualAncestor.html

49. Wikipedia, The Free Encyclopedia, http://en.wikipedia.org/, May 2006

Acknowledgements

First and foremost, I would like to thank my good friends Gary and Michelle Amirault of Tentmaker Ministries (http://www.tentmaker.com), whose faithful efforts over many years have culminated in the absolute best Internet source of historical reference information and texts pertaining to Universal Reconciliation. I would also like to thank my beautiful wife Susan for her listening ear and loving insights about the content of this book. I would be remiss if I did not acknowledge the excellent proof reading and advice received from my good friends Ked Murray and Joe Manning. And last but not least, I want to provide my heartfelt thanks to my dear friends Tim Durham and Tom Tibbetts who challenged me on this all-important element of the Christian faith. Though we see things differently, we do so in undiminished respect and Christian love, just as it should be with different perspectives regarding spiritual matters to which only He holds the answer.

www.ingramcontent.com/pod-product-compliance
Lightning Source LLC
Chambersburg PA
CBHW072003060426
42446CB00042B/1517